R. D. MILLER

# AN
# INTERPRETATION
# OF KANT'S
# MORAL PHILOSOPHY

THE DUCHY PRESS

8 LANCASTER ROAD, HARROGATE

1993

A catalogue record for this book is available
from the British Library

ISBN  0  9511256  5  6

Printed and bound in Great Britian by
Smith Settle
Otley, West Yorkshire

# CONTENTS

CHAPTER ONE

THE FOUNDATIONS
OF THE METAPHYSICS OF MORALS, 1785

Although Kant bases his philosophy on reason
and moral law, he also requires a second principle,
to predispose man to act on moral law.

So we can distinguish in Kant's moral philosophy two archetypal kinds of principle: (a) the
principle of transcendent reason as the presiding
spirit of the noumenal world, producing objective
universal moral laws, absolute in their validity
and authority; (b) an immanent or indwelling moral
principle, a subjective moral disposition, enabling
man to act in accordance with objective moral law.

It is not difficult to recognise the second
type of principle in Kant's description of the "good
will", at the beginning of his first major work of
moral philosophy, the "Foundations". - "Es ist über-
all nichts in der Welt, ja überhaupt auch außer derselben zu denken möglich, was ohne Einschränkung für
gut könnte gehalten werden, als allein ein guter
Wille" (IV.393,LWB.55).

The absolute character of the terms in which
the "good will" is described, the statement that it
is the only thing that can be called good without
qualification, strongly suggest that it is intrinsi-
cally good, that there is, so to speak, an immanent
moral principle within it, and that it does not derive its moral character from any other principle.

In a striking passage Kant brings out the in-
trinsic value of the good will, by declaring that
even if such a will lacked the ability to achieve
its purpose, it would nevertheless, as though by its
own virtue, shine like a jewel, "as something that
has its full value in itself" (IV.394,LWB.56). However, Kant does not imply that it is unimportant
whether the good will does in fact achieve its purpose; nor that the will might justify its existence,
so to speak, simply by cultivating its inner moral
goodness. The good will must make every effort ("bei
seiner größten Bestrebung",ibid); it must summon up

every means at its disposal, in order to make its
own contribution to the good of the world.

In an article by Robert B.Louden on "Kant's
Virtue Ethics" ("Philosophy",61,1986) the critic
argues that, despite the emphasis that Kant places
on "duty", his moral theory is really far more in
agreement with "virtue ethics" than most people suppose. According to this theory, morality should be
concerned less with the performance of separate acts
which conform to moral law, than with the cultiva-
tion of a virtuous character, such as will tend to
produce virtuous actions. R.B.Louden quotes another
critic who points out that "it is noteworthy that
the philosopher who is most completely identified
with the doctrine of stern duty should begin, not
with a statement about what we ought to do, but
rather with a judgment of what is unqualifiedly
good" (Robert Paul Wolff, "The Anatomy of Reason",
New York,1973,56f). In fact, the suggestion that
there is a real connection between "virtue ethics"
and Kant's moral theory, and that the connection is
supplied partly by the concept of the "good will",
is well-founded. On the other hand, if it is true
(as R.B.Louden says) that virtue ethics, generally
speaking, gives natural inclinations a significant
part to play in moral action, then we must make it
clear that this is not true of the kind of virtue
ethics expounded by Kant. The contrast between the
generous praise given by Kant to the "good will",
and his rejection of natural inclinations as morally
worthless, leaves no room for doubt about that.

It is true that there is a certain analogy between a natural inclination and the good will, in
the sense that both represent a subjective disposition; but our description of principle (b), exemplified by the good will, as "a subjective moral principle, enabling man to act in accordance with objective moral law", should make it clear that in Kant's
opinion the good will, if it really is a good will,
is permanently associated with reason and moral law,
in a way that a natural inclination cannot be.

We are told that man has been endowed with
reason, in order that the will may be "governed" by
it (IV.394f,LWB.56). Reason is described as a "practical" faculty, i.e. "a faculty that is to influence
the will" ("d.i.als ein solches, das Einfluß auf den
Willen haben soll",IV.396,LWB.58). Again, we are
told that it is the destiny or function of reason to
produce a will that is good in itself ("so muß die
wahre Bestimmung derselben sein, einen....an sich
guten Willen hervorzubringen",ibid). Thus the good
will, exemplifying principle (b), has an innate compatibility with principle (a), with reason. So the
good will is an indwelling subjective moral principle, which even while it operates spontaneously, at
the same time acts in accordance with reason and
moral law.
    Not only is the good will to be clearly disting-
uished from a natural inclination,but also the will,
as a principle that is "good" and "pure" (IV.393,
LWB.55), has the task of opposing any natural inclination or impulse which does not agree with the
objective requirements of moral law. This task is no
easy one; for the will is itself subject to natural
inclinations. So the concept of the will reflects
the eternal problem in Kant's philosophy, that of
man divided between reason on the one hand, and on
the other nature with its morally unacceptable "inclinations" ("Neigungen"). - "The will stands so to
speak at the parting of the ways,between its 'a priori' principle, which is formal, and its 'a posteri-
ori' impulse, which is material...It will have to be
determined by the formal principle of volition, when
an action is carried out from duty, since every material principle has been withdrawn from it" (IV.400,
LWB.61).
    Even in his own day Kant was criticised by
Schiller for his negative attitude to natural inclinations. But in the present century there has ap-
peared a tendency in a certain type of "revisionist" critic actually to deny that Kant rejects such
inclinations as having no moral worth.

One argument that is sometimes advanced by these critics runs as follows. If a person in carrying out a certain action is motivated, not only by natural inclination, but also by a sense of duty, and if we can believe that the sense of duty would in itself have sufficed to produce the action without the support of any inclination, then the action can be regarded as morally justified. However, the critics sometimes concede that it is hazardous to believe this, unless there is in fact no direct inclination to perform the action. The criticism has the effect of distracting the reader from Kant's outright rejection of natural inclination as a moral motive, by introducing an entirely different question, whether the motive of duty would by itself have produced the action.

At the beginning of the "Foundations" Kant discusses a number of cases to illustrate his method of assessing the moral value of actions, according to whether natural inclination or duty is the motive. In the case of the shopkeeper who carefully avoids overcharging any of his customers, although his conduct is in conformity with duty ("pflichtmäßig"), we cannot conclude that he acts "from duty and principles of honesty". Since he is concerned only with his own advantage in safeguarding his reputation for honesty, we must decide that his action is carried out "neither from duty nor from direct inclination, but merely with a selfish intention" (IV.397,59).

Another way in which revisionists attempt to discount Kant's rejection of natural inclinations, is by maintaining that his aim is simply to point out that it is easier to identify duty as the motive, if there is no evidence that a natural inclination is also playing a part. In fact however Kant's main purpose is to point out that duty alone can be a truly moral motive, and that a natural inclination is morally worthless.

This is made clear in the second example cited by Kant, where he points out that the act of saving one's life might be regarded either as a duty or as an action arising from inclination (the natural fear of death). The difficulty of distinguishing between the two motives does not prevent Kant from passing a very clear verdict, by declaring that the "anxious care with which the greater part of humanity preserve their lives has no moral value, and their maxim has no moral content" (IV.397,59). As a critic has pointed out: "Kant did not say that because we all have an inclination to self-preservation, it is hard to tell whether an act directed to self-preservation has moral worth; he says categorically that it does not" (R.G.H.47). Thus R.G.Henson refutes the assertion of the revisionists that Kant does not really reject natural inclinations as morally worthless. He supports the true view of Kant's moral doctrine, his belief that moral action is based on the rational principle of duty as opposed to the natural principle of inclination. Henson refers to this kind of moral action, in which inclination conflicts with and is defeated by the principle of duty, as the "battle-citation model". So far Henson is on solid ground.

But he goes on to maintain that there is to be found in Kant's later work, "The Metaphysics of Morals" (1797), another type of moral action, which he calls the "fitness-report model", in which he claims that natural inclinations play a part as well as duty. Here he is on less solid ground. It is true that Kant, in "Die Metaphysik der Sitten", refers to certain "aesthetic conditions" ("ästhetische Vorbegriffe der Empfänglichkeit des Gemüts für Pflichtbegriffe", VI.399). In this passage Kant indicates the kind of condition that he has in mind, by referring to "moral feeling", "conscience", "love of one's neighbour", and "self-respect". But far from associating such conditions with natural inclinations, Kant explicitly denies that they are empirical in origin, but maintains that they represent the effect upon us of the moral law. -"Das Bewußtsein derselben ist nicht empirischen Ursprungs, sondern kann nur auf das eines moralischen Gesetzes, als Wirkung desselben aufs Gemüt, folgen" (ibid).

Kant furthermore asserts that such subjective conditions are best induced in us "simply by reason" ("durch bloße Vernunftvorstellung"), and quite apart from any "pathological attraction" ("abgesondert von allem pathologischen Reize", ibid), i.e. not in response to any natural inclination.

We have already examined the first two cases which Kant quotes in order to demonstrate his method of deciding whether an action has moral value or not. We have seen that the shopkeeper, in treating all his customers alike, is motivated only by self-interest; and that the action of the person who preserves his life, in so far as he does so, not from a sense of duty, but from an instinctive fear of death, is morally worthless. In the third case, on the other hand, when an unhappy man overcomes his desire to commit suicide, "not from inclination or fear, but from duty", then his action is indeed of moral value (IV.398,59). So far we have seen that if an action is not carried out from a sense of duty, it is declared to be of no moral value; and the action that is most clearly carried out from a sense of duty, and therefore has moral value, is the one that is opposed to natural inclination (in the case of the person who overcomes his desire to commit suicide).

It is the fourth example that is most instructive, for it is here that Kant undertakes to judge, not a selfish natural inclination, but a generous emotion of the human heart. Natural inclinations tend to fall into two groups, those which in modern parlance might be described as "cooperative" or altruistic, and others which are "antagonistic", that is, self-centred and anti-social. In Kant's day the former type of inclination was described by Rousseau as arising from "pure" natural emotion ("le pur mouvement de la nature",C.E.V.161; or "l'état de nature dans sa pureté",ibid,194). Schiller too distinguished this aspect of human nature from "crude" nature by referring to it as "pure" ("Solange der Mensch noch reine...nicht rohe Natur ist",NA.436).

The fourth case is discussed as follows.-"It is our duty, whenever we can, to do good: and besides there are certain souls so sympathetically disposed, that without any other motive of vanity or egotism, they derive an inner pleasure from spreading joy all about them; and are able to take delight in other people's happiness, in so far as it is their work. But I maintain that in such a case an action of that sort, however it may conform to duty, however kind it may be, nevertheless has no true moral value, but is on a par with other inclinations, for instance the desire for honour, which if by good chance it coincides with what is indeed in the general interest and in conformity with duty, is honourable and deserves praise and encouragement, but not the highest esteem; for the maxim lacks all moral value, that is, the requirement that such actions should be carried out, not from inclination, but from duty" (IV.398,59).

When Kant speaks of the action resulting from natural sympathy (or pure nature) as "conforming to duty", he does not mean that the agent is motivated by a sense of duty as well as by a feeling of sympathy; it is simply that the result may outwardly be the same as that of an action inspired by a sense of duty. Kant certainly seems open to criticism at this point. He assumes that sympathy is not accompanied by a sense of duty; he makes a false distinction between the motive of sympathy, which he rejects as of no moral value, and what he considers to be the true motive of duty. Kant's account of the matter does not agree with our actual experience of what it is like to feel sympathy. If for example we feel, so to speak, that we "really must help", we cannot fail to recognise that our sense of obligation arises not merely from a generous emotion of the heart,but also from our awareness of a moral duty. The philosopher appears to have divided what nature has united.

Kant seems to imply that it is only "by good chance" ("glücklicherweise") if the action of the "sympathetic souls" appears to have moral value, because it happens to correspond to the kind of action

that might have been dictated by a sense of duty.
But we have no reason to assume that a sympathetic
person is without self-awareness, nor that he is incapable of deciding to act on his or her sympathetic
inclination, precisely because it agrees with and
reinforces the sense of duty that is also operative.

It is not the "sympathetic souls" whom Kant
commends, but the "Menschenfreund", the philanthrop-
ist or "friend of man", whose sympathy with others
has been extinguished by some private sorrow, or the
type of person who is cold and indifferent by temperament, because it is they who find the moral
strength to rise above their handicap and to help
others, "not from inclination, but from duty" (IV.
398,59). That is the phrase which Kant so persist-
ently employs in describing these cases, almost as
if he expected and wished to forestall the attempts
of twentieth-century critics to "revise" his text.

Certain critics are inclined to reject any suggestion that Kant, in judging the morality of an action, fails to distinguish between selfish and unselfish inclinations. Yet we have already seen that
his negative attitude to inclinations applies both
to the selfish shopkeeper and to the "sympathetic
souls"; and the same point is brought out in a number of similar passages. There is for example the
following passage in "The Critique of Practical
Reason" (V.118,222). "Inclination is blind and servile, whether it is of the good variety or not".
Elsewhere Kant speaks of "inclinations which degrade
humanity, however they may be decked out" ("Neigungen, die, sie mögen einen Zuschnitt bekommen, welchen sie wollen...die Menschheit degradieren",V.71,
179). Here too Kant maintains that if the will is
determined by "a feeling, of whatever kind it may
be" ("ein Gefühl, welcher Art es auch sei"), then
the ensuing action may conform to moral law, but
will not be carried out for the sake of the law.

We need to be clear about Kant's attitude to
the universal desire for happiness. Most people seek
happiness,the satisfaction of their natural desires,

for its own sake; and their action in doing so is in Kant's opinion without moral value (IV.399,60). But he maintains that it is indirectly the duty of people to safeguard their happiness, since otherwise, burdened with care and worry, they might be tempted to neglect their duties (ibid). Therefore Kant concludes that happiness should be cultivated, not as an end in itself, but as a means to an end, in order that people may be in the right frame of mind to attend to their duties.

Kant's rejection of natural inclinations as having no moral value, is again seen in his remarks on the biblical commandment that we should love our neighbour. He points out that the reference cannot be to love in the sense of inclination, because such love cannot be subject to a moral command. What is referred to is beneficence from the motive of duty, which can lead to the desired conduct "even if there is no motive of inclination, or even if the commandment is opposed by a certain uncontrollable aversion in human nature". At this point Kant could scarcely make the distinction between inclination and duty, feeling and reason, clearer than in fact he does. "Doing good from the motive of duty is practical and not pathological love, love that resides in the will rather than in a propensity of our sensibility, in principles of action rather than in languishing sympathy; the former qualities alone are subject to moral commandments."

"Liebe als Neigung kann nicht geboten werden, aber Wohltun aus Pflicht, selbst wenn dazu gleich gar keine Neigung treibt, ja gar natürliche und unbezwingliche Abneigung widersteht, ist praktische und nicht pathologische Liebe, die im Willen liegt und nicht im Hange der Empfindung, in Grundsätzen der Handlung und nicht schmelzender Teilnehmung; jene aber allein kann geboten werden" (IV.399,60f).

By "pathological" love Kant means love that is based on a natural inclination, and is not under the control of reason. The will on the other hand has the function of "doing good from duty", that is, by acting on rational-moral principlies.

However, Kant's remarks on the commandment that
we should love our "neighbour" are open to criticism. He is right in distinguishing "love" in the
biblical sense of "charity" from natural inclination. But charity is not merely rational, not simply
a process of obeying a moral law, of "doing one's
duty". There is a certain spiritual feeling in such
benevolence; and when Kant says that love cannot be
produced in response to a moral commandment, he appears to overlook a certain aptitude for spiritual
love which is already present in human nature, an
aptitude which people may nevertheless need to be
exhorted to employ for the benefit of their fellow
human beings.

R.G.Henson's interpretation, affirming the importance in Kant's moral theory of "duty" and "reason" as against natural "inclination", has been challenged by the critic Barbara Herman in an article
entitled "On the Value of Acting from Moral Duty"
("The Philosophical Review",90,1981). However, some
of the arguments advanced in this article appear to
be strangely inconsistent with the writer's main
thesis that Kant is not, or at least not always,
opposed to natural inclinations, as lacking moral
value. In particular she appears to support Kant's
case against the "sympathetic souls",who take pleasure in helping people from natural sympathy. She
points out that Kant compares the conduct of the
sympathetic souls with that of people who act from
a desire for honour, a desire which is described as
only "fortunate" if it causes them to hit on something which is to their credit. In other words, it
is Kant's argument, and the critic's too, that natural sympathy is an instinctive reaction, unaccom-
panied by any consideration whether the person who
receives the sympathy is deserving of it, or whether
the action of the agent in sympathising with him is
morally justified. The critic attempts to illustrate
her point by an amusing but rather absurd example.
Supposing that a person plentifully endowed with
such instantaneous sympathy were to "see someone

struggling late at night with a heavy burden at the back door of the Museum of Fine Arts", she suggests that the person concerned might instinctively and unthinkingly assist the very person who might well be engaged in stealing valuable art treasures. The critic comments as follows. "In acting from immediate inclination, the agent is not concerned with whether his action is morally correct or required. That is why he acts no differently, and in a sense no better, when he saves a drowning child than when he helps the art thief." In the critic's opinion, "the man of sympathetic temper, while concerned with others, is indifferent to morality". This is a point that we have already discussed in connection with Kant's remarks concerning the "sympathetically disposed souls". Why should it be assumed that a sympathetic inclination necessarily entails indifference to morality? According to the critic, "if we suppose that the only motive the agent has is the desire to help others, then we are imagining someone who would not be concerned with or deterred by the fact that his action is morally wrong". Well, of course; if you begin by imagining whatever you like of an imaginary character, however improbable, then (at least in theory) he will inevitably act in the way that you imagine that he will act. The fallacy lies in the supposition that sympathy precludes any moral motive. Why should we suppose in the first place that a sympathetic person must be devoid of other moral qualities, such as reason and common sense? Why does the critic assume that there is a high correlation coefficient between sympathy and the kind of unthinking reaction that she describes?

The critic also gives a watered-down version of the case of the "friend of man", discussed by Kant. In the original version the man is not described as "normally" helping others from sympathy, but "sometimes when his feelings are dimmed" as helping them from duty. Kant describes the man as undergoing a personal tragedy, which even as it deprives him of his natural tendency to sympathise, at the same time

teaches him that "action performed without any inclination, but solely from duty,alone has true moral
worth". The point that is made is, not that the man
acts from duty because he lacks natural sympathy,
but that the motive of duty that he discovers in
himself, is of much greater moral value than natural
sympathy. The critic also comments that the case of
the friend of man "does not imply that no dutiful
action can have moral worth if there is cooperating
inclination. Nor does it imply that a sympathetic
man could not act from the motive of duty when his
sympathy was aroused". As regards the first assertion, Kant almost invariably speaks of natural inclination as adulterating the pure motive of duty;
and since he rejects the actions of the "sympathetically disposed souls" as "lacking any true moral
value", it is difficult to see how he could welcome
any cooperation between even the better type of
natural inclination and duty.

As regards the second point, it is the critic
herself who, in her comments concerning the "sympathetic souls", has implied that "a sympathetic man
could not act from the motive of duty when his sympathy was aroused", as witness her reference to the
kind of instantaneous unthinking sympathy (without
any sense of duty, as she maintains) that might well
motivate a person who rescues a child from drowning.

When the critic says that "overdetermined actions" (by which she means actions in the performance
of which the agent is motivated by natural inclination as well as by his sense of duty) "can have moral worth so long as the moral motive has priority
over the satisfaction of inclination", she attributes to Kant a doctrine which he certainly does not
mention in "The Foundations". In fact he makes it
clear that he is opposed to it. For instance,in discussing the "respect" which the will should have for
the moral law, he emphasises that the respect must
be "pure" (it must be "reine Achtung" for the law);
which means that any natural inclination, to which
we might be tempted to yield, must be rejected. He

explicitly states that "an action from duty must altogether exclude the influence of inclination, and
with it every object of the will" ("Nun soll eine
Handlung aus Pflicht den Einfluß der Neigung und mit
ihr jeden Gegenstand des Willens ganz absondern",IV.
400,61). In acting on a moral law we must repudiate
any inclination ("mit Abbruch aller meiner Neigung-
en",IV.401,62). So the "Achtung" or respect which
the will is under an obligation to pay to the moral
law, at the same time entails its ability to dissociate itself from any natural inclination.

When Kant says that, once the influence of inclinations has been eliminated, there remain only
two principles which determine the will: the objective principle of the moral law, and the subjective
principle of "pure respect" for the law, he is referring to the two archetypal principles of which we
spoke at the beginning of this chapter.The "respect"
which the will has for the moral law exemplifies
principle 'b', the subjective principle which dis-
poses the will to act in accordance with the moral
law. In a footnote to IV.401,62. Kant makes certain
valuable observations concerning this principle. We
tend to think of respect as a sign of humility,prop-
erly adopted in deference to some person or principle exalted above us. So, in the footnote, Kant refers to respect as "the consciousness of the subordination of my will to the law" ("das Bewußtsein der
Unterordnung meines Willens unter einem Gesetze").
He also says that "respect is really the idea of a
value which diminishes my self-love" ("Eigentlich
ist Achtung die Vorstellung von einem Werte, der
meiner Selbstliebe Abbruch tut").

However, it gradually becomes clear that Kant's
thoughts concerning respect are not only centred on
the subordination of the will to moral law; on the
contrary, they lead to the most important idea in
"The Foundations", that of the autonomy of the will.

By feeling respect for the law, we so to speak
assimilate it and make it our own. Kant implies that
we identify ourselves so closely with the rational

law that we virtually impose it on ourselves. -"Der
Gegenstand der Achtung ist also lediglich das Gesetz
und zwar dasjenige, das wir uns selbst und doch als
an sich notwendig auferlegen" (ibid). Perhaps we
might say that if the will were not a good will, if
there did not exist a certain affinity between the
will on the one hand, and reason and moral law on
the other, the will would be no more capable of res-
ponding to the law than a stone is capable of res-
ponding to the sound of beautiful music.

When Kant says that the law is "in itself necessary", he means that we cannot arbitrarily make the
law whatever we please: it must conform to reason.
Since the law is the law, we are subject to it,with-
out considering our self-love; but as imposed on us
by ourselves, it is an effect of our will. From the
first perspective, it has an analogy with fear, from
the second with inclination.-"Als Gesetz sind wir
ihm unterworfen, ohne die Selbstliebe zu befragen;
als uns von uns selbst auferlegt, ist es doch eine
Folge unsers Willens, und hat in der ersten Rücksicht Analogie mit Furcht, in der zweiten mit Neigung." If the law is simply imposed on us, without
our willing it, then we feel something in the nature
of fear. This is the stern code of morality,with the
emphasis on "duty", that is sometimes regarded as
typical of Kant's philosophy. If on the other hand
we "impose the law on ourselves", by willing it, by
acting of our own volition, in that case we feel
something in the nature of "inclination". We have
seen that Kant rejects natural inclinations as having no moral value, since they belong to the world
of empiricism, of "natural necessity". When he says
that the experience of imposing a law on ourselves
is analogous to that of feeling an "inclination" to
do something,he means that there is a certain voluntarism in a moral action that we perform in imposing
a moral law upon ourselves. Kant not only rejects
natural inclinations as morally worthless: he at the
same time introduces another kind of "inclination",
a moral inclination,a principle that it is advisable

to refer to by some other expression, for instance
"disposition", lest it should be confused with a
natural inclination. It is in fact the selfsame moral disposition to which we have already referred as
the archetypal principle (b). In the footnote Kant
is careful to distinguish between the two sorts of
"inclination". A natural inclination belongs to the
empirical world; it is a feeling of desire for some
object in the natural world. The feeling of "respect" on the other hand is not a feeling that has
been received through some outer influence; on the
contrary it has been "self-induced" by a rational
concept.-"Allein wenn Achtung gleich ein Gefühl ist,
so ist es doch kein durch Einfluß empfangenes, sondern durch einen Vernunftbegriff selbstgewirktes Gefühl...". Thus the idea of "respect" for moral law
is used by Kant as a means of introducing the idea
of the autonomy of the will, a further stage in the
exemplification of principle (b). When Kant refers
specifically to "duty" as "the necessity of an action from respect for the law", he adapts the idea of
duty to the principle of autonomy; for he now speaks
of duty in reference, not to an imposed law, but to
a law that is voluntarily acted on by virtue of the
respect that the will feels for it.

We have seen that the critic Barbara Herman and
other revisionists tend to give the false impression
that in Kant's opinion a natural inclination might
well cooperate with the will in support of reason
and moral law. On the contrary, he sets the two
principles over against each other, as mutually antagonistic. He says that the respect which we feel
for the moral law far outweighs the value that we
attach to a natural inclination ("...daß es eine
Schätzung des Wertes sei, welcher allen Wert dessen,
was durch Neigung angepriesen wird, weit überwiegt",
IV.403,64). He deplores what he refers to as a "natural dialectic", i.e. "a tendency to cavil at the
strict laws of duty and their validity, and at least
to cast doubt on their purity and strictness, and if
possible to adapt them to our wishes and inclinations, i.e. to corrupt them fundamentally" (IV.405).

He commends the "pure idea of duty, unadulterated by the admixture of any empirical inducement" ("die reine und mit keinem fremden Zusatze von empirischen Anreizen vermischte Vorstellung der Pflicht",IV.410, 70). He makes the most explicit references to his aversion both to natural inclinations themselves,and to "a mixed moral philosophy consisting of motives of feelings and inclinations, and at the same time of rational concepts (IV.411,71).

In contrast to the incompatibility between natural inclination on the one hand, and reason and moral law on the other, we notice the correspondence between the subjective principle of the will (if it is a good will) and the objective principle of the moral law with which reason is associated. To the transcendent principle of lawfulness present in reason there is added a corresponding immanent principle of lawfulness in the will, which enables it, not only to feel respect for moral law, but also to take appropriate moral action spontaneously. Whenever Kant refers to the two principles, we notice a tendency for him to speak of the will in terms of freedom and spontaneity, as well as in terms of its "lawfulness". This is important, because it shows that the impulse to act in agreement with the moral law springs from the will itself. So in one passage, where Kant asks whence we derive our idea of God and the greatest good, he replies: "Simply from the idea of moral perfection formed by reason, an idea that is inseparably associated with that of a free will" ("Lediglich aus der Idee, die die Vernunft a priori von sittlicher Vollkommenheit entwirft und mit dem Begriffe eines freien Willens unzertrennlich verknüpft",IV.409,68).

We must now examine a passage in which the agreement between the will and reason is described as adversely affected by the fact that the former is distracted by natural inclinations and selfish interests. -"Ein jedes Ding der Natur wirkt nach Gesetzen. Nur ein vernünftiges Wesen hat das Vermögen, nach der Vorstellung der Gesetze, d.i. nach

Prinzipien, zu handeln, oder einen Willen. Da zur
Ableitung der Handlungen von Gesetzen Vernunft er-
fordert wird, so ist der Wille nichts anders als
praktische Vernunft. Wenn die Vernunft den Willen
unausbleiblich bestimmt, so sind die Handlungen
eines solchen Wesens, die als objektiv notwendig
erkannt werden, auch subjektiv notwendig, d.i. der
Wille ist ein Vermögen nur dasjenige zu wählen, was
die Vernunft unabhängig von der Neigung als praktisch notwendig, d.i. als gut, erkennt. Bestimmt
aber die Vernunft für sich allein den Willen nicht
hinlänglich, ist dieser noch subjektiven Bedingungen (gewissen Triebfedern) unterworfen, die nicht
immer mit den objektiven übereinstimmen; mit einem
Worte, ist der Wille nicht an sich völlig der Vernunft gemäß (wie es bei Menschen wirklich ist): so
sind die Handlungen, die objektiv als notwendig
erkannt werden, subjektiv zufällig, und die Bestimmung eines solchen Willens objektiven Gesetzen
gemäß ist Nötigung; d.i. das Verhältnis der objektiven Gesetze zu einem nicht durchaus guten Willen
wird vorgestellt als die Bestimmung des Willens
eines vernünftigen Wesens zwar durch Gründe der Vernunft, denen aber dieser Wille seiner Natur nach
nicht notwendig folgsam ist" (IV.412,72).

"Everything in nature works according to laws.
Only a rational being has the ability to act according to the idea of laws, that is, according to principles; or (in short, such a being has) a will.
Since reason is required for the deduction of actions from laws, the will is nothing but practical
reason. If reason unfailingly determines the will,
the actions of such a being which are recognised to
be objectively necessary are also subjectively necessary, i.e. the will is a faculty of choosing only
what reason independently of inclination recognises
as practically necessary, i.e. as good.But if reason
for its own part does not determine the will ade-
quately, if the latter remains liable to subjective
conditions (certain impulses) which do not always
agree with the objective conditions; in a word, if

the will in itself is not completely in accord with
reason (as is the case with human beings): then the
actions which objectively are recognised as necessary, are subjectively contingent, and the determination of such a will according to objective laws is
constraint; i.e. the relation of the objective laws
to a will that is not thoroughly good is to be regarded as the determination of the will of a rational being, to be sure by principles of reason, to
which however the will by its very nature is not
necessarily amenable."

It becomes clear in this passage that if principle (a), i.e. reason and moral law, requires the
cooperation of an associated principle, that principle is not natural inclination, but on the contrary principle (b), the indwelling moral disposition, exemplified by the good will. When Kant speaks
of reason as recognising a certain action as "practically necessary", that is, as morally good, reason
does so "independently of inclination" ("unabhängig
von der Neigung"). Moreover, if anything prevents
the will from enjoying the ideal relation that it is
capable of having with reason, it is the "subjective
conditions (certain impulses)", that is, natural inclinations (to which the will is subject) that di-
vorce the will from reason and bring about the need
for "constraint" ("Nötigung"), exercised by reason
on a will that is "not completely good".

In contrast to this unhappy state of affairs,
sometimes brought about by our inclinations, we are
also given a convincing impression of the ideal relation between reason and the good will. The latter,
we are assured, is able to act according to the idea
of laws, that is, principles. The will that deduces
actions from laws,is described as "nothing but practical reason". We note the agreement, the harmony,
between reason and the will, in the statement that
when reason completely determines the will, the objective necessity of the actions approved by reason,
is matched by a subjective necessity in the will.
Nothing could bring out more clearly the affinity

that exists between the will and reason, than the
statement that the former "chooses" to do what the
latter pronounces to be morally good. If it is a
question of "choice", this makes it clear that the
will, in acting in accordance with reason, at the
same time acts of its own volition. Thus Kant brings
out the spontaneity that the will exhibits in its
relation with reason and moral law. Even when he
speaks of the occasions when the will is not altogether, by its very nature, amenable to the principles of reason, even in such passages we are able,
if we take into account the unfortunate influence of
natural inclinations, to appreciate the ideal relation which the will, if it were immune to such inclinations, would be able to enjoy with reason.

    Kant has now made it clear that an "imperative",
the distinguishing feature of which is, so to speak,
an "ought" ("ein Sollen",413,72), becomes necessary
only when the will is not determined by an objective
law of reason, as though by "its own subjective
character" ("seiner subjektiven Beschaffenheit nach",
ibid). We see the importance that Kant attaches to
the subjective contribution made by the will.Ideally
the "subjective" faculty of the will (principle b)
should spontaneously cooperate with the "objective"
principle of reason. But if it is to do so, it must
acquire something of the "objectivity" of reason. It
must not act simply from subjective motives, but
must act objectively, from motives that are valid
for every rational being (ibid). So at this point
Kant distinguishes between what is merely "pleasant"
and what is morally good. The former pleases this or
that person by affecting his feeling (his "Empfindung") and thus influencing his subjective condition;
the latter, based on rational principles, influences
the will in a way that is valid for everyone (ibid).
Here again we see that it is not a natural inclination, but the will, to which Kant attributes the
ability to acquire a certain objective validity,
corresponding to that of reason.

    In a remarkable footnote (413,73) Kant seeks to

explain how the will runs a risk of losing its spontaneity and independence, a risk which may arise in
either of two ways. On the one hand, he points out
that the will may come to be influenced by natural
inclination; it is perhaps for this reason that he
refers to the will, at this point, as the "Begehr-
ungsvermögen", the faculty of desire. In this case
the will is subject to a certain "need" (a "Bedürfnis"). Kant compares this first kind of dependence,
on natural inclination, with another kind, which
arises when the will, which is not always, by its
very nature ("von selbst") in agreement with reason
("der nicht von selbst jederzeit der Vernunft gemäß
ist"), is persuaded to act in agreement with reason,
only by a certain adventitious "interest", that is,
not for the sake of reason itself.

It is not surprising that Kant should object to
the tendency to misuse reason as a means of satisfying a natural inclination ("da nämlich die Vernunft
nur die praktische Regel angibt, wie dem Bedürfnisse
der Neigung abgeholfen werde", ibid). However, the
fact that he compares this misuse of reason with the
other misuse, which arises when the will is not, by
its very nature, in harmony with reason, but when
reason has to employ "constraint" (a kind of "interest") to force the will to conform to moral law –
this shows the importance that he attaches to the
spontaneity of the will, and to its voluntary cooperation. The two faults are of course related. It is
because the will is not thoroughly attuned to reason
and moral law, that it is subject to natural inclinations; and it is on account of the latter tendency
in the will, that reason is obliged to resort to
constraint in the case of a recalcitrant will.

The constraint that has to be applied by reason
becomes necessary only when the will, distracted as
it is by certain sensuous impulses, fails to work in
harmony with reason. The predominant idea is not
constraint, but the moral principle immanent in the
will. Although that principle cannot always be relied on, the qualifications which Kant introduces at

every turn in his criticism of the will (not "completely" in conformity with reason, not "thoroughly"
good, not "necessarily" amenable) show that he is
anxious to represent its inherent morality as the
ideal which he cherishes. The will, by its very nature, has at least the potential for acting on moral
law of its own volition. From time to time a case
occurs in which the will fails to act according to
reason, and a moral imperative has to be applied.
But behind such a case, in which "constraint" has to
be employed, hovers the ideal of a correspondence or
affinity between the moral disposition of the subjective will, and the moral law of reason. Indeed
Kant actually envisages just such a case, in which
a "wholly good will" acts in accordance with the
objective law of morality, without the need for
any constraint to be exerted upon it; "because, of
itself, by its own subjective character, it can only
be determined by the idea of the good". -"Ein vollkommen guter Wille würde also eben sowohl unter objektiven Gesetzen (des Guten) stehen, aber nicht dadurch als zu gesetzmäßigen Handlungen genötigt vorgestellt werden können, weil er von selbst nach
seiner subjektiven Beschaffenheit nur durch die Vorstellung des Guten bestimmt werden kann" (414,73).

Only in the case of God, or in that of a "holy"
will can this ideal be fully realised; for any imperative, any idea that something "ought" to be,
would be quite inappropriate if applied to God, "because volition is already, of itself, necessarily in
agreement with the law". -"Daher gelten für den
göttlichen und überhaupt für einen heiligen Willen
keine Imperativen; das Sollen ist hier am unrechten
Orte, weil das Wollen schon von selbst mit dem Gesetz notwendig einstimmig ist" (ibid).

Kant represents the ideal, that is, the perfect
agreement of "volition" with the moral imperative,
as attainable only by God. But it may be that by his
reference to a "holy" will he wishes to imply that
it is an ideal for which man himself should strive.

In view of what Kant refers to as the "subjective

imperfection of the will", that is, the fact that the will is sometimes subject to natural inclination, a moral imperative is needed to correct that imperfection. -"Daher sind Imperativen nur Formeln, das Verhältnis objektiver Gesetze des Wollens überhaupt zu der subjektiven Unvollkommenheit des Willens dieses oder jenes vernünftigen Wesens, z.B. des menschlichen Willens, auszudrücken" (413,73).As Kant says, the subjective maxims of the will are sometimes opposed to the objective principles of practical reason (ibid). Yet almost in the same breath he associates a morally good action,not only with practical reason, but also with the "principle of a will which is in some manner good" ("So sind alle Imperativen Formeln der Bestimmung der Handlung, die nach dem Prinzip eines in irgend einer Art guten Willens notwendig ist" (ibid). Again, in discussing a categorical imperative (which relates to an action which is good in itself, and not merely as a means to an end, as in the case of a hypothetical imperative), he describes such an action as "necessary in a will which is in itself conformable to reason".

"Wird (die Handlung) als an sich gut vorgestellt, mithin als notwendig in einem an sich der Vernunft gemäßen Willen, als Prinzip desselben, so ist er kategorisch" (ibid).

In other words, in such passages Kant shows that he is anxious to associate the will with the moral legislation of practical reason. In the case of a hypothetical imperative, which merely supplies the means which must be adopted to attain a certain end, the role played by the will is merely a part of an analytic process, since the imperative "extracts the idea of necessary actions for this end out of the very idea of the willing of this end" (417,76). The imperative that is associated with the universal desire for happiness is of this nature; for the end, happiness, is known, and all that is required is to derive from this end the means by which it may be attained (416,75).

In the case of a categorical imperative, there is no end or object from which the imperative can be

derived (419,78). The categorical imperative is a
"synthetic-practical proposition a priori" (420,79).
At this point Kant adds the following passage in a
footnote. "To the will, without any presupposed condition, I attach the deed a priori, therefore necessarily (although only objectively, i.e. subject to
the idea of reason, which would have complete control of all subjective motives)." Kant adds the following explanation. "This is therefore a practical
proposition, which does not analytically deduce the
willing of an action from any other presupposed (act
of will)...but which connects (the willing of the
action) with the idea of the will of a rational being directly, as something that is not contained in
it" (i.e.the presupposed act of will).

However involved this footnote may seem, Kant
is simply drawing attention to a distinction between
two processes. If we simply decide on an action (b),
which will satisfy a natural inclination (a), then
action (b) is merely analytic in the sense that it
is really contained in the natural inclination (a),
and therefore does not enable us to escape from natural necessity. If on the other hand we decide to
act on a moral principle,then this means two things.
First, it is 'a priori', in the sense that it is not
deduced from an empirical motive such as natural inclination. Second, it is synthetic in the sense that
it is not merely deducible analytically from some
principle belonging to the natural world, but adds
something new to that world, a moral principle. In
this context "analytic" refers to an action of the
will that is derived from a natural inclination; and
"synthetic" refers to an action that is not deduced
by analysis of a natural inclination, but is deduced
'a priori' from a principle of reason. Kant, in this
passage,once again excludes natural inclination from
his moral system; at the same time he exalts the
will in its moral capacity, principle (b), far above
natural inclination.

Since the categorical imperative, as distinct
from the hypothetical imperative, is not limited by

any condition that it must satisfy a natural inclination, it simply affirms the general validity or
universality of a moral law. So Kant states the
first formula of the categorical imperative, the
formula of universal law.

"Handle nur nach derjenigen Maxime, durch die
du zugleich wollen kannst, daß sie ein allgemeines
Gesetz werde." (421,80)

"Act only according to that maxim, through
which you can at the same time will that it should
become a universal law."

A maxim is a subjective rule of conduct, in
agreement with which the will decides to act. There
are all sorts of maxims, some morally good, others
morally bad. In the first formula of the categorical
imperative Kant tells us to act only on the kind of
maxim that is suitable to be regarded as a moral
law. Kant calls it a "universal" law, because whereas a hypothetical imperative, when acted on, may enable this or that person to satisfy his immoral inclination or his motive of self-love, a moral law on
the other hand is valid as a precept or guide to
moral conduct for all people and in all situations.

Kant does not only tell us to choose a maxim
which is suitable to be a moral law. We must also be
able to will that it should become a universal law.
The same point is brought out in an earlier version
of the first formula.

"Ich soll niemals anders verfahren als so, daß
ich auch wollen könne, meine Maxime solle ein allgemeines Gesetz werden." (402,63)

"I am never to proceed otherwise, than in such
a way that I can also will that my maxim should become a universal law."

The "good will", introduced at the beginning of
this work, exemplifies principle (b), the subjective
moral principle which cooperates spontaneously with
reason and objective moral law, principle (a). It is
good "an sich" ("in itself"). The demand that the
will should act morally comes from the will itself.
The acceptance of a duty ("Ich soll", "I am to") is

matched by the insistence of the will itself that it should be free to "will" ("daß ich auch <u>wollen könne</u>") that its maxim should become a universal law. Kant certainly speaks of the categorical imperative as concerned with "duty" (he refers to it as the "universal imperative of duty", "der allgemeine Imperativ der Pflicht",421,80). But it is not simply imposed on the will; on the contrary, it is written into the various formulae that it is to be "willed" by that faculty.

It is rather strange that the formula of universal law should be followed by the law of universal nature.

"Handle so, als ob die Maxime deiner Handlung durch deinen Willen zum allgemeinen Naturgesetze werden sollte" (ibid).

"Act in such a way, as though the maxim of your action were to become, through your will,a universal law of nature."

Possibly Kant considers that the formula of the "universal law of nature", which depends on the analogy provided by the universality of the laws of the natural world, might be easier for the average person to understand than the categorical imperative. At any rate he uses the new formula in commenting on the four types of "duty" that he now discusses. These duties fall into two groups, consisting of duties to ourselves and duties to others, that is,"perfect and imperfect" duties. In a footnote (421,81) Kant makes clear his continued rejection of natural inclination, by explaining that by a "perfect duty" he means one which "allows no exception in favour of inclination" ("diejenige, die keine Ausnahme zum Vorteil der Neigung verstattet").

The first case is that of a man who, finding that life causes him more suffering than happiness, has to decide whether the maxim that he is inclined to adopt, that in these circumstances he should commit suicide, would be suitable as a universal law of nature. In a similar case that Kant examined earlier (397f,59), he approved of the man's decision that suicide would be contrary to his duty, since it is his duty to preserve his life. He makes the same judgment in the present case (422,81), but he does so by arguing that a maxim tending to destroy life could not be adopted as a law of nature which exists to promote life. This is one way of looking at the matter, but when Kant judged the man's proposed action by reference to his duty (397f,59), he came to the same conclusion by means of a higher principle than that of nature, namely, the principle of reason.

In the second case Kant considers whether a person would be justified in borrowing money and in promising to repay it, without having any intention of doing so. The person concerned has to consider whether, if he made such conduct his maxim, it could ever be accepted "as a universal law" (or, as the text says later, as a "universal law of nature",422). Of course the answer is that the maxim could not be adopted as a universal law; but the reason that is given is far from satisfactory. Kant simply argues that if everyone made such a false promise, no one would believe it, and it would become impossible to borrow money in that way. The true answer, of course, is that such conduct would not conform to moral law, nor would it be in the best interest of society.

The third case concerns a man who makes it his maxim to neglect the talent with which he has been endowed, and to give himself up to a life of pleasure. Could this maxim be made a universal law? The answer that is given is that "nature could still exist in accordance with such a universal law", but it is implied that it would be an existence at a very low moral and intellectual level.

"Er kann unmöglich wollen, daß dieses ein allgemeines Naturgesetz werde...Denn als ein vernünftiges Wesen will er notwendig, daß alle Vermögen in ihm entwickelt werden" (423,82).

"He cannot possibly will that this should become a universal law of nature...For as a rational being he necessarily wills that all his faculties should be developed in him."

Despite his reference to the law of nature, Kant in this instance has to appeal to the law of reason as supplying a better criterion for judging such a case. At this point it seems as though Kant were using the reference to the law of nature in such a way as to throw into relief the very different law of reason. Nature could, somehow or other, still exist, if people neglected their talent and gave themselves up to a life of pleasure, but at a very much lower level than it would be if they lived in accordance with the universal law of reason.

We must not overlook the importance of Kant's statement that the man who neglects his talent cannot possibly will that this should become a universal practice. In this third case discussed by Kant it appears that, even though the maxim (that one is justified in neglecting one's talent for the sake of a life of pleasure) might be acceptable as a universal law of nature, nevertheless the will itself, using its own independent judgment as a rational being, must necessarily decide that such a maxim should not be adopted as a universal moral law; therefore it cannot "will" it. This agrees with the increasing importance which Kant is giving to the part played by the "will", particularly with respect to its autonomy.

In the fourth case discussed by Kant, the will itself again appears to rise above the standard that satisfies the universal law of nature. Would a person be justified in making it his maxim, to refuse to give a fellow human being the help that he needs? Would such a maxim be acceptable as a universal law of nature? The answer given by Kant is as follows.

"Obgleich es möglich ist, daß nach jener Maxime ein allgemeines Naturgesetz wohl bestehen könnte: so ist es doch unmöglich, zu wollen, daß ein solches Prinzip als Naturgesetz allenthalben gelte"(423,82).

"Although it is possible that a universal law of nature, based on that maxim, might exist, nevertheless it is quite impossible to will that such a principle should be universally valid as a law of nature."

If the person, despite his natural inclination to refuse to give a fellow human being the help that he needs, nevertheless cannot bring himself to will that such selfishness should become a universal law of nature, this shows (a) that his will is superior to his natural inclination, and (b) that it is possible, as in the third example, that the independent judgment of his will is superior to that of a person who simply applies the criterion of the universal law of nature. However, Kant's last word on the subject seems almost to rule out the possibility that what he is suggesting is an independent will, spontaneously making a superior moral judgment; for on the contrary, what he finally suggests is that a person who rejected such a selfish maxim as unsuitable to be adopted as a universal law of nature, might himself be acting from a selfish motive, because if he were to recommend such a law, he himself might be denied help, if he were ever in need of it. Of course it might also be implied that it is only by imagining what it would be like in his case, if he underwent the experience of needing help without being able to get it, that he comes to realise that it would be wrong to put other people in the same position. But if Kant implies this, he does not actually say it.

After considering the tendency of people to adopt maxims based on natural inclinations (maxims which are quite unsuitable to be adopted as universal moral laws), Kant dwells on the conflict between the natural inclinations to which man is subject, and the moral side to his nature. If, he says, we act on a maxim that is opposed to our moral duty, it is not because we wish our maxim to become a universal law. We recognise our maxim as morally wrong, but we wish to make an exception in our case in favour of our inclination."As on the one hand we regard our action from the point of view of a will that is entirely conformable to reason,but then on the other hand from the point of view of a will that is affected by inclination, there is really no contradiction here; but there is a resistance of inclination to the precept of reason (antagonismus), whereby the universality of the principle (universalitas) is converted into a mere generality (generalitas), by which the practical principle of reason is intended to meet the maxim halfway" (424,83). Kant's point is precisely that reason must not meet the maxim (based on natural inclination) halfway. He therefore warns us that our conduct must be in conformity with the categorical imperative, which "every human will" must recognise as the law. -"Denn Pflicht soll praktisch-unbedingte Notwendigkeit der Handlung sein; sie muß also für alle vernünftige Wesen...gelten und allein darum auch für allen menschlichen Willen ein Gesetz sein" (ibid). As we would expect, in this confrontation between reason and natural inclination, the will is on the same side as reason. Only if it were affected by natural inclination, would the will be false to its commitment to reason and moral law. "Whatever is derived from the special natural character of man, whatever is characteristic of certain feelings and propensity...that can give us a maxim, but no law; a subjective principle, to act in conformity with which we have the necessary propensity and inclination, but not an objective principle,in accordance with which we are instructed to act, even though all our propensity, inclination and natural character is against it; so that the sublimity and inner dignity of the commandment would be demonstrated all the more clearly by a duty, the less the subjective motives were for it, the more they were against it, without on that account diminishing in the least the compulsion exercised by the law, or depriving it of any of its validity."

"...daß es um desto mehr die Erhabenheit und innere Würde des Gebots in einer Pflicht beweiset, je weniger die subjektiven Ursachen dafür, je mehr sie dagegen sind, ohne doch deswegen die Nötigung durchs Gesetz nur im mindesten zu schwächen und seiner Gültigkeit etwas zu benehmen" (425,84).

Not even the most ardent revisionist could hope to deny, on the basis of this passage, that Kant repudiates natural inclinations as incompatible with moral law. Indeed, he glories in the fact that they serve only to throw into relief the "sublimity and inner dignity" of the law, with which the will is associated. Philosophy, says Kant, must be on its guard to defend its values against the false moral teaching based on natural inclination. "Here it must demonstrate its purity ("Lauterkeit") as a force that is to preserve its own laws, not as the herald of those which are whispered into its ear by an innate "sense", or by who knows what guardian spirit of nature, which...can never produce principles dictated by reason" (ibid). "Everything that is empirical is not only quite unsuitable as an accessory to the principle of morality, but also highly deleterious to the purity of morals themselves" (426,84). Kant deprecates the tendency of reason, in its weariness, to recline on the pillow of empiricism, and in a dream of sweet illusions to substitute for true morality a "bastard" moral philosophy based on "experience" (426,84f).

We have seen that it is an essential part of the first formula of the categorical imperative that if a maxim is to be adopted as a universal moral law, it must be approved by the will as suitable to fulfil that function. Kant gives added emphasis to this part played by the will, in a later passage.

"Man muß wollen können, daß eine Maxime unserer Handlung ein allgemeines Gesetz werde: dies ist der Kanon der moralischen Beurteilung derselben überhaupt" (424,82).

In describing this function, which is fulfilled by the will, of deciding whether a maxim can be willed to become a universal law, as "the canon (or criterion) of moral judgment", Kant considerably enhances the authority of the will. From this point of view the "good will", principle (b), is engaged in the same work as that for which reason itself, principle (a), is responsible, that of moral legislation. We have seen that reason, through the moral laws that it formulates, acquires a certain quality of "sublimity and inner dignity" (425,84). But we are also told that the "good will" itself, by freeing human behaviour from empiricism and contingency, acquires a "sublime" value that is above price ("der eigentliche und über allen Preis erhabene Wert eines schlechterdings guten Willens",426,84).

Unfortunately the reference to the "sublime" value of the good will has been omitted in some translations; for instance in one version the passage has been translated as "the proper and inestimable worth of an absolutely good will". Of course it is understandable that the reader should not associate the will with sublimity, since sublimity is generally attributed to reason, rather than to the will. Nevertheless the whole trend of Kant's thought in this part of the "Foundations" is to exalt the will to a level almost equal to that of reason itself, in accordance with the principle of the autonomy of the will.

In fact Kant has now practically arrived at this idea. -"Here it is a question of the objective practical law, hence of the relation of the will to itself, so far as it determines itself merely by reason, since everything which is related to what is empirical naturally falls away."

"Hier aber ist vom objektiv-praktischen Gesetze die Rede, mithin von dem Verhältnisse eines Willens zu sich selbst, so fern er sich bloß durch Vernunft bestimmt, da denn alles, was aufs Empirische Beziehung hat, von selbst wegfällt" (427,85).

It is unfortunate that Abbott at this point is not altogether reliable; for after the reference to the "relation of the will to itself", he then speaks of the will as "determined by reason alone". Kant himself says that the will is "a faculty of determining itself for action in conformity with the idea of certain laws". -"Der Wille wird als ein Vermögen gedacht, der Vorstellung gewisser Gesetze gemäß sich selbst zum Handeln zu bestimmen" (427,85). For good measure he then refers to the "self-determination" (the "Selbstbestimmung") of the will.

There are two aspects of the principle of self-determination. On the negative side, the will is free from empirical influences, from natural inclinations; and on the positive side, it determines itself by means of the objective, universal laws of reason. Kant has already introduced the idea of autonomy, without actually naming it, but "self-determination" is practically synonymous with "autonomy", that is, the idea that the will determines itself by means of the laws of reason.

Kant deals first with an idea closely related to "self-determination" and "autonomy" - the idea that man is an end in himself, and must always be treated as such, and not simply as a means for whatever purpose another man might wish to use him.

"Nun sage ich: der Mensch und überhaupt jedes vernünftige Wesen existiert als Zweck an sich selbst, nicht bloß als Mittel zum beliebigen Gebrauche für diesen oder jenen Willen" (428,86).

The underlying assumption is that man is an end in himself, because the will, which has "absolute value", is the "source of definite laws", indeed of a categorical imperative. -"Gesetzt aber, es gäbe etwas, dessen Dasein an sich selbst einen absoluten Wert hat, was als Zweck an sich selbst ein Grund bestimmter Gesetze sein könnte, so würde in ihm und nur in ihm allein der Grund eines möglichen kategorischen Imperativs,d.i. praktischen Gesetzes,liegen."

Kant contrasts the absolute value that a rational being has as an end in himself, with the merely "relative" or "conditional" value which is all that the object of a natural inclination has. It is for this reason, Kant says (428,86), that it is the universal wish of every rational being to be rid of natural inclinations. The purposes or ends with which man as a rational being is properly concerned are the "objective" moral purposes - "things, the existence of which is a purpose in itself" (ibid).

It is because every rational being realises that he shares his rational nature with all other rational beings,who are likewise capable of producing laws

or principles by which they determine how they shall
act, that he understands that they too must be regarded as ends-in-themselves.

So Kant produces another formula for the categorical imperative, the formula of man as an end-in-
himself. "Act in such a way as to treat humanity,
both in your own person, as in every other person,
always as a purpose, never as a means."

"Handle so, daß du die Menschheit sowohl in
deiner Person, als in der Person eines jeden andern
jederzeit zugleich als Zweck, niemals bloß als Mittel brauchst" (429,87).

The moral principle immanent in the autonomous
will leads, not only to the formula of man as an
end-in-himself, but also to the concept of a "kingdom of ends" ("ein Reich der Zwecke",433,91). If the
kingdom is to come about, each will must act, not on
subjective impulses which relate only to itself, but
from objective motives, valid for every rational
being (427,85). There are these two aspects of the
will in the kingdom of ends: it acts spontaneously
and of its own volition, yet it acts in accordance
with objective laws, valid for every rational being
and every will. It is the fact that each will has,
immanent within it, an autonomous principle enabling
it to form moral laws, which qualifies it to act "as
a lawgiving member in the kingdom of ends" ("ein gesetzgebend Glied im Reiche der Zwecke",435,92). The
moral principle immanent in the autonomous will is
the basis of the correspondence between the inner
world of the will and the outer world of objective
and universal law, i.e. the "compatibility" of the
maxims of the will of every rational being with the
process of universal lawgiving ("diese Schicklich-
keit seiner Maximen zur allgemeinen Gesetzgebung",
438,95).

Kant now reverts to the four "duties", which he
has already judged by the criterion of the universal
law of nature (421,80), and proceeds to consider
each of the duties in the light of his latest formulation of the categorical imperative, the formula of

man as an end in himself. In the first case, in which
a man considers suicide because he finds his life
scarcely bearable, Kant's verdict, according to his
new formula, is that the man, in committing suicide
despite his duty to preserve his life, would be making that duty conditional upon his willingness or
unwillingness to endure his present unhappiness
(429,87). In the second case Kant points out that if
you borrow money from another person, and falsely
promise to repay it, you are using that other person
as a means to an end (ibid). In the third case, if
we were to neglect what talent we have, for the sake
of a life of pleasure, this would scarcely promote
the idea of man as an end in himself (430,88). In
the fourth case, if we were to refuse to help other
people, when they are in need of help, this too
would demonstrate that we do not regard those people
as ends in themselves (ibid).

Kant now sets out to explain the importance
that he attaches to the idea of the autonomy of the
will, that is, the "idea of the will of every rational being as a universally lawgiving will" ("die
Idee des Willens jedes vernünftigen Wesens als eines
allgemein gesetzgebenden Willens",431,89). His explanation is that "the will is not only subject to
the law, but subject to it in such a way that it
must be regarded as itself lawgiving, and only on
that account as subject to the law (of which it can
consider itself the author)".

"Der Wille wird also nicht lediglich dem Gesetze unterworfen, sondern so unterworfen, daß er
auch als selbstgesetzgebend und eben um deswillen
allererst dem Gesetze (davon er selbst sich als Urheber betrachten kann) unterworfen angesehen werden
muß."

But we still need to know why it is only because
the will has produced the law, that it can be regarded as subject to the law. The answer is given in
the following passage.

"Denn wenn wir einen solchen denken, so kann,
obgleich ein Wille, der unter Gesetzen steht, noch

vermittelst eines Interesse an dieses Gesetz gebund-
en sein mag, dennoch ein Wille, der selbst zu oberst
gesetzgebend ist, unmöglich so fern von irgend einem Interesse abhängen..." (432,89).

"Although a will which is subject to laws, can
still be bound to this law by means of an interest,
nevertheless a will which is itself a supreme lawgiver, cannot possibly depend upon an interest in
this way."

Perhaps we should have said that the answer is
only partly given in this passage. For Kant at this
point, like the skilful author of a detective story,
keeps the reader on tenterhooks by delaying the complete explanation of the mystery as long as he can.
Meanwhile we are left with unanswered questions.What
is meant by an interest? Why can one person be bound
to the law by an interest, although another person,
the "lawgiver" cannot?

In speaking of "a will which is subject to laws",
Kant is referring to a will which is not itself a
lawgiver. According to Kant such a will can be bound
to the law, not for the sake of the law, but only by
means of some adventitious "interest". Only if the
will has itself acted as lawgiver can it be bound to
the law in the true sense, that is, for the sake of
the law. Kant takes his explanation a stage further
in the following passage. -"Also würde das Prinzip
eines jeden menschlichen Willens, als eines durch
alle seine Maximen allgemein gesetzgebenden Willens,
wenn es sonst mit ihm nur seine Richtigkeit hätte,
sich zum kategorischen Imperativ darin gar wohl
schicken, daß es eben um der Idee der allgemeinen
Gesetzgebung willen sich auf kein Interesse gründet
und also unter allen möglichen Imperativen allein
unbedingt sein kann" (432,90).

"So the principle of every human will, giving
universal laws in all its maxims,would be very suitable as a categorical imperative. Because of the
idea of universal lawgiving, it is based on no
interest; and so, of all possible imperatives, it
alone can be unconditional."

From this we understand that although a person
normally needs some inducement (an "interest") before he will obey a moral law, the person who has
actually worked out the law for himself needs no
such inducement to obey it, because he is already
committed to it.

We must now examine a passage which greatly
strengthens the case which Kant makes out for basing
his system of morality, not only on a transcendent
moral law imposed so to speak from above, but on
a moral law which at the same time originates in a
moral principle immanent in the will itself. -"Es
ist nun kein Wunder, wenn wir auf alle bisherige Be-
mühungen, die jemals unternommen worden, um das Prinzip der Sittlichkeit ausfindig zu machen, zurück-
sehen, warum sie insgesamt haben fehlschlagen müss-
en. Man sah den Menschen durch seine Pflicht an Gesetze gebunden, man ließ es sich aber nicht einfall-
en, daß er nur seiner eignen und dennoch allgemein-
en Gesetzgebung unterworfen sei, und daß er nur verbunden sei, seinem eignen, dem Naturzwecke nach aber
allgemein gesetzgebenden Willen gemäß zu handeln.
Denn wenn man sich ihn nur als einem Gesetz (welches
es auch sei) unterworfen dachte: so mußte dieses
irgend ein Interesse als Reiz oder Zwang bei sich
führen, weil es nicht aus seinem Willen entsprang,
sondern dieser gesetzmäßig von etwas anderm genötigt
wurde, auf gewisse Weise zu handeln. Durch diese
ganz notwendige Folgerung aber war alle Arbeit,
einen obersten Grund der Pflicht zu finden, unwieder-
bringlich verloren. Denn man bekam niemals Pflicht,
sondern Notwendigkeit der Handlung aus einem gewiss-
en Interesse heraus. Dieses mochte nun ein eigenes
oder fremdes Interesse sein. Aber alsdann mußte der
Imperativ jederzeit bedingt ausfallen und konnte zum
moralischen Gebote gar nicht taugen. Ich will also
diesen Grundsatz das Prinzip der Autonomie des Willens im Gegensatz mit jedem andern, das ich deshalb
zur Heteronomie zähle, nennen" (432,90).

"Looking back now at all the previous attempts
that were ever undertaken to discover the principle

of morality, it is not to be wondered at that all were destined to fail. It was seen that man was bound to laws by duty, but it did not occur to people that the laws to which he is subject are only those which he has himself produced, though they are at the same time universal; and that he is only obliged to act in conformity with his own will, which is however intended by Nature to produce universal laws. For whenever he was considered to be subject only to some law, no matter what it might be, this law had to be provided with some "interest", by way of attraction or compulsion, because it did not arise as a law from his own will, but this will was compelled by some other law to act in a certain way. Through this quite inevitable result, however, all the labour that was devoted to finding a supreme principle of duty was irretrievably wasted. For it was never duty that was discovered, but only the necessity of acting from a certain "interest", no matter whether this was the will's own interest or not. As a result the imperative could never be anything but conditional, and was quite unsuitable as a moral command. So I will call this the principle of the autonomy of the will, in contrast to all others, which I therefore describe as heteronomy."

We must compare this passage with the quotation from 412,72. In the earlier passage (supra p.16f), although the spontaneous and voluntary character of the will, and the moral law that is immanent in the will, are certainly brought out, two other points are also stressed: firstly, the fact that the will cannot always be relied on to fulfil its potential for moral goodness, and secondly that the remedy for this failure of the will is "Nötigung" (constraint) exercised by reason. Thus the emphasis in the first of the two passages tends to rest on the transcendent principle of reason, rather than on the moral principle immanent in the good will.

In contrast to this description of a will that has failed to fulfil its moral potential, in the second passage Kant discusses the disadvantage of

being subject to a law other than the law which one
has given to oneself (i.e. the disadvantage of being
determined by a law that is imposed on the will, as
distinct from the law produced by the will itself).

The basis of Kant's argument is the belief that
unless the will wholly identifies itself with the
law to which it is subject, the latter can neither
be "unconditional", nor can it be an "imperative";
and that the will can wholly identify itself with
the law, only if it has itself acted as lawgiver,
only if it has produced the law on which it acts. If
the law is imposed on the will by transcendent reason as an act of "Nötigung" (constraint), the will
can be prevailed upon to obey the law, not by the
law itself, but only by means of some adventitious
"interest", i.e. an inducement in the form of an
"attraction" or "compulsion" ("Reiz oder Zwang").
These "interests" or inducements deprive the will of
any claim to be "unconditional" ("unbedingt"). Perhaps we may paraphrase Kant's somewhat paradoxical
but convincing conclusion, by saying that in his
view the only duty that a man can be made to fulfil
unconditionally,is the duty that he himself resolves
to fulfil; and that the only law which he can be
forced to obey absolutely, is the law that arises
spontaneously from his own will ("weil es...aus
seinem Willen entsprang"). Not only should it not be
necessary for transcendent reason to apply constraint to the will (if the latter overcomes the
temptation to yield to its natural inclinations),
but it is also desirable that such constraint should
not be applied, since it is self-defeating. The law
that arises from the will itself is not only more
spontaneous than imposed law; it is also more likely to be unconditional.

The comparison between the two passages also
brings out another important difference.In the first
passage it is because the will is subject to certain
"subjective conditions or impulses", that is,natural
inclinations, that "constraint" has to be applied by
reason and moral law. So in this passage the point

is made that the will must be independent or "autonomous" with respect to natural inclinations.

In the later passage, on the other hand, Kant
points out that the moral law should not be simply
imposed on the will by transcendent reason, but that
it should arise spontaneously from the will itself.
In this passage, therefore, Kant points out that the
will must be autonomous with respect to transcendent
reason.

But there is an important difference between
these two aspects of the autonomy of the will. When
Kant refers to the autonomy of the will with respect
to natural inclinations, he is concerned with an
inherent incompatibility between the autonomous will
and natural inclinations. The autonomy of the will
with respect to reason, on the other hand, does not
imply any such inherent incompatibility between the
two. Reason and the will are natural allies; indeed
the latter, as we have seen, is actually referred to
in terms of "practical reason". The will exercises
freedom and autonomy even while cooperating with
reason, by demonstrating that reason should not be
imposed externally on the will.

As a result of the greater importance that is
attached to the autonomous moral principle immanent
in the good will, the admired attributes of reason
are seen, as the work progresses, to belong also to
the will. Kant extends the range of these attributes
from transcendent reason, principle (a), to the will
itself, principle (b).

Not only reason, but the will too is described
as a "lawgiver". As we have already seen, it is re-
referred to as "self-lawgiving" ("selbstgesetzgebend",431,89), and as "universally lawgiving" ("all-
gemeingesetzgebend",ibid). To the autonomous will is
also attributed yet another quality borrowed from
reason – its "dignity", which as Kant observes (434,
92), is to be ascribed to "a rational being that
obeys no law other than that which at the same time
it gives".-"Die Vernunft bezieht also jede Maxime
des Willens als allgemein gesetzgebend auf jeden

anderen Willen...und dies zwar...aus der Idee der
Würde eines vernünftigen Wesens, das keinem Gesetze
gehorcht als dem,das es zugleich selbst gibt"(ibid).

As we have already seen (supra p.31), not even
"sublimity" is denied to the will; but when the reference to "sublimity" is omitted in translation,
both the quality of sublimity and the fact that this
quality has been extended from reason to the will,
are lost. In the pages that succeed that all-import-
ant passage (432f,90) Kant continues to hammer home
the vital part played in moral lawgiving by our
"own" will, as he has already done in the passage
itself by his reference to man's "own" lawgiving
("seine eigene...Gesetzgebung"), his acting in accordance with his "own lawgiving will" ("seinem eigenen...gesetzgebenden Willen gemäß"), and the mistake made in requiring a person to act on a law
"that has not sprung as a law from his will" ("weil
es nicht als Gesetz aus seinem Willen entsprang").
In the following passage, although Kant refers to
the unfortunate case in which the "duty" of acting
according to moral law has to be imposed on the will
by the use of "constraint", he also refers to the
more fortunate case in which there is a natural
agreement between the maxims of the will and the
moral law. "If the maxims are not already, by their
very nature and of necessity, in agreement with the
objective principle of rational beings, as universally lawgiving, then the necessity of acting on
that principle is practical constraint, i.e. duty"
(434,91).

It is clear that the idea which Kant cherishes
in such a passage is the condition in which the
will, "by its very nature and of necessity", is in
agreement with the objective moral principles of
reason, and that "constraint" and the call of "duty"
are required only when not all is as it should be
with the will (subject as it is from time to time to
the effect of selfish motives and crude impulses).
Kant in this passage seems to imply that there is no
need for "duty" if the maxims of the will agree with

objective law; and he is thus using the expression
in reference to duty imposed by transcendent reason.
But it would be true to say that we should continue
to think of duty as in fact a duty, even when it is
self-imposed by a will acting in agreement with objective moral law.

It is not only the "unconditional" quality, the
"dignity" (the universally lawgiving quality), and
the "sublimity", that are extended from reason to
the will: in addition "respect" is also said to be
due, not only to reason, but to the will itself. In
the footnote to 401,62. we are told that "the object
of respect is solely the law", but Kant adds that
the law that he has in mind is "the law that we impose on ourselves,though it is necessary in itself".
-"Der Gegenstand der Achtung ist also lediglich das
Gesetz und zwar dasjenige, das wir uns selbst und
doch als an sich notwendig auferlegen." He also men-
tions that the law that we impose on ourselves is
the work of the will ("eine Folge unsers Willens").
Finally, in a passage that succeeds the second of
the two key passages, Kant declares that "our own
will...is the real object of respect" (so far as it
produces universal laws).

"Unser eigener Wille...ist der eigentliche Gegenstand der Achtung" (440,97).
The importance which Kant attaches to principle (b),
the indwelling moral principle, exemplified as it is
by the good will, is brought out very clearly in the
passage where he states that "the will whose maxims
necessarily agree with the laws of autonomy, is a
holy will, an absolutely good will".

"Der Wille, dessen Maximen notwendig mit den
Gesetzen der Autonomie zusammenstimmen,ist ein heiliger, schlechterdings guter Wille" (439,96).

The same idea is expressed at greater length in
an earlier passage. -"Ein vollkommen guter Wille
wäre also eben sowohl unter objektiven Gesetzen (des
Guten) stehen, aber nicht dadurch als zu gesetzmäßigen Handlungen genötigt vorgestellt werden können, weil er von selbst nach seiner subjektiven

Beschaffenheit nur durch die Vorstellung des Guten
bestimmt werden kann. Daher gelten für den göttlich-
en und überhaupt für einen heiligen Willen keine
Imperativen...weil das Wollen schon von selbst mit
dem Gesetz notwendig einstimmig ist" (414,73).

"A completely good will would be subject just
as much to objective moral laws, but could not be
represented as compelled to take lawful actions, because in accordance with its own subjective character, it can be determined only by the idea of what
is morally good. Therefore imperatives have no validity for a divine or a holy will...because volition
of itself is necessarily in agreement with the law."

Kant's brilliant exposition (432,90) of the
virtues of the moral principle immanent in the autonomous will, does much to justify another formula
of the categorical imperative, the formula of autonomy itself. -"Diese Gesetzgebung muß aber in jedem
vernünftigen Wesen selbst angetroffen werden und aus
seinem Willen entspringen können,dessen Prinzip also
ist: keine Handlung nach einer andern Maxime zu tun,
als so, daß es auch mit ihr bestehen könne, daß sie
ein allgemeines Gesetz sei, und also nur so, daß der
Wille durch seine Maxime sich selbst zugleich als
allgemein gesetzgebend betrachten könne" (434,91).

"Lawgiving must be present in every rational
being; it must arise from his will, according to the
principle: act only on a maxim that may properly
form a universal law, in such a way that the will by
its maxim may at the same time regard itself as producing a universal law."

In view of the support given to it in 432,90,
this must be regarded as the most striking and important of all the formulations of the categorical
imperative, and as the basis of the other formulae.

It seems that certain critics do not find it
easy to accept the idea of autonomy as an attribute
of the will. After considering the key passage in
which Kant gives the most convincing exposition of
this idea, they sometimes dismiss it with a comment
suggesting that it represents a kind of aberration

to which the philosopher is subject from time to time, and from which he cannot free himself. Moreover, certain critics (failing to understand that the two main formulations of the categorical imperative are virtually identical) are perplexed by the way in which Kant alternates, as they suppose, between the view of moral law as a principle which binds the will absolutely, and the view of it as arising from the will itself. There is a suggestion here that the principle of the autonomy of the will runs counter to the absolute authority of the objective moral law as produced by reason. Yet any fear that the critics might have lest the autonomy of the will might challenge the authority of moral law based on reason is in fact groundless. As we have already seen, the formula of universal law and the formula of autonomy are completely in agreement with each other, since both speak of "universal law", and both refer to the person concerned as "willing" that his maxim should become a universal law. Kant has made it very clear in the two key passages, that it is only when the moral imperative arises, in accordance with the principle of autonomy, from the immanent or indwelling moral disposition of the will, that it can be "unconditional" or absolute.

Kant himself deprecates the notion that the two formulae are opposed to each other, and at the same time he underlines the prior importance of the formula of autonomy. -"Allein daß gedachtes Prinzip der Autonomie das alleinige Prinzip der Moral sei, läßt sich durch bloße Zergliederung der Begriffe der Sittlichkeit gar wohl dartun. Denn dadurch findet sich, daß ihr Prinzip ein kategorischer Imperativ sein müsse, dieser aber nichts mehr oder weniger als gerade diese Autonomie gebiete" (440,97).

"That the principle of autonomy in question is the sole principle of morals, can be readily shown by pure analysis of the concepts of morality; for in this way we find that its principle must be a categorical imperative, and that what this commands is nothing more nor less than this very principle of autonomy."

There are times when the "categorical" character of the imperative is associated with "Nötigung"
or constraint, which appears to be opposed to auto-
nomy.But this becomes necessary only when the will's
desire for the "object" has itself introduced heteronomy; that is, the object imposes its law on the
will and so negates the will's own moral law. The
moral imperative is "categorical", not only in the
sense that it is unconditional and is sometimes
associated with "constraint", but also because it
frees the will from the "hypothetical" imperative of
its heteronomous dependence on the object. The hypothetical imperative, which states that such and such
an action must be carried out if the desired object
is to be gained, is replaced by the categorical imperative, which lays it down that a certain action
must be performed unconditionally, in order that the
moral law may be fulfilled. Thus the categorical
character of the imperative, far from endangering
the autonomy of the will, is on the contrary a guar-
antee of its restored autonomy.

Another factor which begins to play a significant part in the "Foundations" is the "Gesinnung",
the moral disposition, which Kant regards as the
principle which constitutes what is essentially good
in a moral action ("Das Wesentlich-Gute derselben
besteht in der Gesinnung", 416,76). He means that it
is the moral disposition that enables a person to
act for the sake of the moral law. If we speak of a
moral principle immanent in the will, we do not mean
simply that the will acts on laws which (through its
own reason) it has produced for itself; rather we
mean that in some inscrutable way the universal
moral laws of reason also operate at the "lower"
level of the will; just as we say that God is immanent in nature, and in the souls of men. To explain
how the will is capable of acting on moral laws
which properly belong to the transcendent world of
reason, it does not suffice to say that reason is
present in each will, so that in acting on moral law
the will acts autonomously on its own reason. The

problem is to explain how a "good will", which even though it possesses reason, cannot be wholly equated with reason (because it is subject to crude and selfish inclinations), can nevertheless in some mysterious way come to accept and act on moral law. It is not simply a matter of pointing out that the will has the means (that is, reason) of giving the law; for reason would be of no avail if the will lacked the inner motive to produce the law. To formulate and act on moral law, it must be a "good" will, with the appropriate moral disposition.

Kant, in his remarks on this principle, includes in his eulogy, not only its "inner worth", but also an impressive list of outward achievements, which serve to enhance its inner worth (the "Vermehrung ihres innern Werts" to which he refers, 439,96).

"Und was ist es denn nun, was die sittlich gute Gesinnung oder die Tugend berechtigt, so hohe Ansprüche zu machen? Es ist nichts Geringeres als der Anteil, den sie dem vernünftigen Wesen an der allgemeinen Gesetzgebung verschafft und es hiedurch zum Gliede in einem möglichen Reiche der Zwecke tauglich macht, wozu es durch seine eigene Natur schon bestimmt war, als Zweck an sich selbst und eben darum als gesetzgebend im Reiche der Zwecke, in Ansehung aller Naturgesetze als frei, nur denjenigen allein gehorchend, die es selbst gibt und nach welchen seine Maximen zu einer allgemeinen Gesetzgebung (der es sich zugleich selbst unterwirft) gehören können" (435, LWB.93). -"And what is it then, which justifies the morally good disposition, or virtue, in making such lofty claims? It is nothing less than the share that it procures for the rational being in universal legislation, and thus makes it eligible to become a member in a possible kingdom of ends, for which it was already destined by its own nature, as an end in itself, and for that very reason as legislating in the kingdom of ends, free with respect to all natural laws, obeying only those laws which it itself has made, and according to which its maxims are able to form part of a universal legislation (to which at the same time it conforms)."

So Kant, in praising the achievements of the morally good disposition, which like the good will represents principle (b), the subjective moral principle, contrives to include practically all the formulae of the categorical imperative (the formula of universal law, the end in itself, the kingdom of ends, and the law of autonomy), in a catalogue of the outer achievements of this inner principle. Thus the good will is succeeded by the good disposition (the "Gesinnung"), which plays a not less important part in representing principle (b) in Kant's "Critique of Practical Reason".

# CHAPTER TWO

## THE CRITIQUE OF PRACTICAL REASON, 1788

Kant, in the first part of this work (the "Analytic"), is engaged in a bridge-building operation between two worlds which he is committed to keeping eternally apart.

Just as in Kant's speculative philosophy the forms of space and time have no meaning except in reference to our perception of the world, so in his moral philosophy his aim is to show that practical reason can determine the will to act morally in the world (V.15,LWB.129). In a passage in which Kant explains his idea of "immanence", he points out that it is the moral law which first gives reason objective practical reality, converting its transcendent use to an immanent one, that is, "in the field of experience".

"Denn das moralische Gesetz beweist seine Realität dadurch...daß es einer bloß negativ gedachten Kausalität...positive Bestimmung, nämlich den Begriff einer den Willen unmittelbar...bestimmenden Vernunft, hinzufügt und so der Vernunft zum erstenmale objektive, obgleich nur praktische Realität zu geben vermag und ihren transzendenten Gebrauch in einen immanenten (im Felde der Erfahrung durch Ideen selbst wirkende Ursachen zu sein) verwandelt" (V.48, LWB.158).

It is in the empirical world, the world of experience, that the rational-moral law is to be put into operation; yet it is from this selfsame world that Kant is inclined to recoil, lest the pure rational character of the moral law should be contaminated by empiricism, by human nature. Any suggestion that there might exist "in the field of experience" a certain moral principle immanent in human nature (one thinks of Rousseau's and Schiller's principle of "pure nature"), a principle that might be able to serve as the ally of reason, with which it might have a certain affinity, is rejected on the ground that such an empirical principle would simply have the effect of watering down reason, and of producing

"reason conditioned by empiricism" ("empirisch be-
dingte Vernunft",V.15,LWB.129). Kant refers here to
the moral freedom that is associated with reason,
freedom which can only be weakened if it is affected
by the "natural necessity" which is held to be characteristic of the empirical world; but it is also
implied that "feelings" and "inclinations", through
which natural necessity works, are inimical to the
pure rationalism of the moral law. We have already
seen that Kant, from a moral point of view, rejects
all "feelings" as empirical. But we have also noted
the attempts made by certain revisionist critics to
deny the fundamental character of Kant's objection
to natural inclinations. We come across the same
tendency in remarks made by critics about Kant's
attitude to "inclinations" in the present work. For
example it has sometimes been maintained that, although Kant sometimes appears to cold-shoulder natural inclinations, this is only because he wishes to
keep clearly in mind the distinction between such
inclinations on the one hand, and on the other the
duties imposed by moral law. For this purpose, it is
sometimes said, he tends to dwell on the extreme
cases, in which the two things,duty and inclination,
are at cross purposes. But Kant does not deal just
with extreme cases. The case of the sympathetically
disposed souls (in the "Foundations") is scarcely an
extreme case of a natural inclination that is obviously without moral value. Kant's purpose is not
simply to distinguish between the claims of duty and
inclination. His objection to natural motives rests
on doctrinal grounds, on his belief that feelings,
belonging as they do to the empirical world, are
subject to natural necessity, and should therefore
play no part in moral considerations.

We have seen that in the "Foundations" the
division between reason and nature is present in the
will itself; for the will belongs both to the world
of nature (because it is subject to natural inclinations), and also to that of reason and the moral
law, since it exemplifies principle (b), the subjective moral disposition. Now in the "Critique" the

division is highlighted by the fact that two distinct expressions are employed to describe the will,
according to whether it is to be regarded as a truly
moral principle or is represented as subject to natural inclination. To take an example, Kant says that
"autonomy of the will" ("Autonomie des Willens") is
the sole principle of all moral laws; "heteronomy of
of the will" ("Heteronomie der Willkür") is opposed
to the principle of the morality of the will ("der
Sittlichkeit des Willens entgegen" (V.33,LWB.144).
So, generally speaking, Kant uses "Wille" in reference to the autonomous will, and "Willkür" in reference to the will that is subject to natural inclinations. But Kant, in employing these expressions,
does not always keep to the distinction which in
general he observes; for instance, in another passage, he refers to the "Autonomie der Willkür"(V.36,
LWB.148).

Critics who seek to exonerate Kant from the
charge that he adopts a negative attitude to natural
inclinations, do so from the best of motives. They
imagine that they are doing Kant a service by rescuing him from the reputation of being an advocate of
a morality of austerity. But to misinterpret a moral
system can never do its author any good. We may not
altogether agree with Kant's negative attitude to
natural inclinations, but our first duty is to give
a true account of his moral philosophy.

In the "Foundations" it is precisely as a result
of its resistance to the blind instinctive character
of natural inclinations that reason acquires the
"sublimity and dignity" that is characteristic both
of reason and of the moral law which it produces
(IV.425,LWB.84). But it is not only reason which
towers above the world of natural inclinations. The
heteronomous influence of the latter is also opposed
by the good will, principle (b), which (when it is
true to itself) supports reason in its task of opposing natural inclinations. Ideally the moral disposition immanent in the will comes to represent the
very principle of autonomy, by supplying an inner

moral impulse, and by <u>choosing</u> only what reason regards as practically necessary. The will supplies
that moral spontaneity which Kant has in mind when
he speaks of it as "determining itself" for action
in the spirit of the moral law.

But there is also one other aspect of the autonomy of the will, which Kant has brought out. There
is more than one principle of autonomy. Even if we
confine ourselves to the autonomy of the will, we
find that there are two aspects of this particular
autonomy. In the first place the will enjoys autonomy in the sense that it is autonomous vis-à-vis
the heteronomy of nature (i.e.natural inclinations).
But secondly, we have seen that the will, as it is
described in the "Foundations", also enjoys autonomy
in the sense that it possesses a certain independence vis-à-vis transcendent reason. The two cases
are very different: whereas the will, in a case in
which moral principles are concerned, is (or should
be) opposed to natural inclination on principle, it
is allied with reason. The will must of course act
in agreement with reason and the moral laws produced by reason. But if the will is compelled to act
on a law that is imposed on it, then it will do so,
not for the sake of the law, but on account of the
constraint to which it is subjected. Only if the
will acts on a law that it has itself produced, can
it obey the law "unconditionally", in accordance
with the principle of the autonomy of the will vis-
à-vis transcendent reason. So the will must aspire
to act autonomously, not only with respect to nature, but also with respect to reason. In the "Foundations", as we have seen, it is above all the autonomy of the will with respect to reason that is
brought out. That particular autonomy of the will is
implied in all the formulations of the categorical
imperative, and it is specifically referred to both
in the formula of universal law and in the formula
of autonomy itself.

In the "Critique of Practical Reason" the warn-
ings given by Kant against the danger that the will

might be determined by natural inclination, rather than by the moral law, are if anything still more urgent than in the "Foundations". Reason must determine the will by means of a practical law, not by means of an intervening feeling of pleasure or displeasure, and not even by a feeling of pleasure in the law itself. As before, the will must act on maxims suitable to be made a universal law, not on selfish or self-indulgent maxims. The autonomy of the will, which is described as "the sole principle of all moral laws" (V.33,LWB.144), depends upon its independence of "any desired object", and on its being determined solely by the form of universal law. The will becomes heteronomous when it becomes dependent on natural law; and instead of giving itself the law, it borrows the assistance of reason in pursuing "pathological" aims (ibid). Returning to the theme of the "sympathetically disposed souls", mentioned in the "Foundations", Kant explains that, instead of simply acting from a certain natural feeling of sympathy, they should seek to act on a moral principle, requiring them to expand their self-love, so as to include a concern for the happiness of others (34f, 145f). In a reference to the "moral sense" theory, according to which the consciousness of virtue is associated with contentment and pleasure, and that of vice with uneasiness and pain, Kant points out that such feelings are the result, not the cause, of the way we behave, whether virtuous or vicious; and that they therefore cannot help us to choose virtue rather than vice (38,150). Kant agrees that if we obey a moral law, we are rewarded with a feeling of satisfaction; this is in fact the true "moral feeling"; but the action itself is produced by a sense of duty. Kant agrees that we should in this way cultivate such a feeling of contentment with ourselves, so long as we remember that the action which gives us this contentment was performed in obedience to a moral law produced by reason. When Kant adds that the virtuous action could not have been produced by a mere "mechanical play of finer inclinations, contending from time to time with coarser ones" (ibid), he is of course reminding us that, from an ethical point of view, natural inclinations, whether of the refined or of the coarse variety, are all highly suspect.

We have seen that Kant, in the "Foundations", tended to concentrate on the autonomy of the will, and maintained that the will must be autonomous even with respect to reason itself, i.e. that it must not be subject to any constraint exercised (as it tended to be in earlier philosophies) by reason upon it; since such constraint would prevent moral action from being unconditional, in the sense that it would be performed, not for the sake of the moral law itself, but as a result of constraint. Now, in the second "Critique", starting with the section, "Of the Deduction of the Principles of pure practical Reason" (V.42,152), Kant widens the concept of autonomy to include, not simply the autonomy of the will, but also that of reason itself.

"Diese Analytik tut dar, daß reine Vernunft praktisch sein, d.i. für sich, unabhängig von allem Empirischen, den Willen bestimmen könne, und dieses zwar durch ein Factum, worin sich reine Vernunft bei uns in der Tat praktisch beweiset, nämlich die Autonomie in dem Grundsatze der Sittlichkeit, wodurch sie den Willen zur Tat bestimmt."

In this passage Kant maintains that practical reason demonstrates its autonomy in two ways: by its independence of everything that is empirical, and by the fact that it determines the will to take moral action. So the will is subsumed under the principle of reason, which is autonomous by virtue of the fact that, far from being subject to natural inclination, it can prevail upon man (though he also belongs to the natural order) to behave morally. The principle of autonomy, in the "Critique of Practical Reason", is based very much on the belief that reason is able to impose its moral will on the sensible world (the "Sinnenwelt",V.43,153). As far as rational beings are concerned, the purpose of reason is to establish a "supersensuous" world, in which "those rational beings can exist in accordance with laws which are independent of all empirical conditions, and which consequently belong to the autonomy of pure reason" (ibid). We see what an impressive image Kant conjures up by means of the image of a principle of reason confronting sensuous nature and so to speak redeeming it (our expression, not Kant's) by means of its autonomous principle of moral law. It is an image which, in the "Deduction of the Principles of pure practical Reason", he seeks to enhance by comparing the part played by practical reason with that which, in the "Critique of Pure Reason", he has described speculative reason as playing. Speculative knowledge is in fact incapable of supplying anything more than the mere intuitions of space and time, limited as these intuitions are to the empirical world, and without reference to the autonomous world of moral freedom (42,153). Kant says that "supersensuous nature", by which he means the existence of beings who, although rational, also belong to the natural order, is distinguished from that natural order by the fact that such rational beings are "independent of all empirical conditions, and therefore belong to the autonomy of pure reason".

"Die übersinnliche Natur eben derselben Wesen ist dagegen ihre Existenz nach Gesetzen, die von aller empirischen Bedingung unabhängig sind, mithin nichts anders als eine Natur unter der Autonomie der reinen praktischen Vernunft" (43,153). So Kant contrives to throw the work of practical reason into relief,by setting it off against the lesser achievement of speculative reason, in supplying the mere forms of space and time in the physical world.

But there is another way in which practical reason is seen to excel, when it is compared with speculative reason. The latter is capable of taking account of the fact that every object in the physical world can cause an effect in another object, and that the first object has itself been subject to an earlier effect caused by a third object. Indeed, speculative reason can go further than this.Although

it must recognise that causality in the physical
world can never be unconditional, it is nevertheless
aware that for every series of conditions there must
necessarily be something unconditional, i.e. a causality capable of determining itself, completely on
its own initiative ("von selbst", 48,158). Although
in the physical world everything is conditioned by
a cause in an infinite series of causes, it is possible for speculative reason, by means of a process
of analysis, to arrive at the idea of the possibility of "absolute spontaneity". -"Daher war die Idee
der Freiheit als eines Vermögens absoluter Spontaneität nicht ein Bedürfnis, sondern, was deren Mög-
lichkeit betrifft, ein analytischer Grundsatz der
reinen spekulativen Vernunft" (48,158).

But here again Kant is concerned to illustrate
the superior part played by practical reason. As far
as speculative reason is concerned, the idea of the
"unconditional" or "absolute spontaneity" is a mere
possibility, an unknown something, or as Kant refers
to it, a "vacant place" (49,159). "This vacant place
reason now fills with a definite law of causality in
an intelligible world (through freedom), namely the
moral law." -"Diesen leeren Platz füllt nun reine
praktische Vernunft durch ein bestimmtes Gesetz der
Kausalität in einer intelligibelen Welt (durch Freiheit), nämlich das moralische Gesetz, aus" (ibid).

In the section entitled "Of the Right of Pure
Reason to an Extension in its Practical Use which is
not possible to it in its Speculative Use" (50,160),
Kant is concerned with the resolution of the third
antinomy. Kant has two purposes. Naturally he aims
to disprove the antithesis, that all causes fall under the law of nature, because that would rule out
the belief that moral law produced by reason represents the principle of spontaneous causality. At the
same time, by vindicating the thesis, he aims to
raise that principle far above the level of nature,
and to show that it is man's true destiny to achieve
moral autonomy, particularly in so far as it implies
freedom from the heteronomy of natural inclinations.

The resolution of the antinomy is achieved by showing that the thesis is true of "noumena" or "things in themselves", and by limiting the antithesis to "phenomena" or "appearances". At this point it is clear that even the revisionists are obliged to admit that dualism is an essential part of Kant's moral philosophy. But they cannot bring themselves to admit that Kant, by committing himself to a philosophy based on the principle of moral autonomy in the noumenal world, at the same time (as far as morality is concerned) repudiates the heteronomous influence exercised by natural inclinations in the phenomenal world.

According to Kant, Hume failed in his theory of causality, precisely because he overlooked the distinction between things in themselves and mere phenomena. By mistaking the objects of experience for things in themselves, he failed to see how one such object could produce a necessary effect in another. Therefore he rejected the idea of causality and replaced it with the subjective idea of "habit" or custom. Against the background of Hume's failure to explain the idea of causality by means of an empirical philosophy, Kant allows a note of triumph to arise, as he declares that "in the concept of a will the idea of causality is already contained; and consequently in that of a pure will the concept of causality with freedom, i.e. one that is not determinable according to the laws of nature".

"Im Begriffe eines Willens ist der Begriff der Kausalität schon enthalten,mithin in dem eines reinen Willens der Begriff der Kausalität mit Freiheit, d.i. die nicht nach Naturgesetzen bestimmbar...ist" (55,164).

Kant proceeds to honour man, as a being who is endowed with free will, by conferring upon him an appropriate Latin title ("Nun ist der Begriff eines Wesens, das freien Willen hat, der Begriff einer 'causa noumenon'"); at the same time emphasising that such a being, in view of his origin, is "independent of all sensuous conditions"("von allen sinnlichen Bedingungen unabhängig", ibid).

If we compare this description of the will that is both "pure" and "free", with the account in the "Foundations" of the autonomous will (in the key passage in IV.432f,90), we notice a difference of emphasis. In the "Foundations" the emphasis is on the moral principle immanent in the will itself, a principle by virtue of which the will is autonomous, not only with respect to natural inclination, but also with respect to a tendency of reason to impose the moral law on the will in an authoritarian way. In the present passage in the "Critique", on the other hand, the will is itself associated with the autonomy of reason vis-à-vis the whole world of nature and natural inclinations.

The subject of the second section of the "Analytic", "Concerning the Concept of the Object of pure practical Reason" (57,166) follows on naturally from Kant's description of a pure will as containing the concept of "causality with freedom". Whatever subject Kant discusses, we notice again and again that it is likely to involve the danger that the will might be determined by natural inclination. The object referred to here is the kind of object to which the will is likely to be attracted by the desire for pleasure. The will should be determined by a law of reason, and reason was not given to man, in order that he might use it as a means of pursuing an object of pleasure (as instinct is used by an animal). If the law directly determines the will, then the ensuing action will be good; but if the will is first determined by an object of pleasure or displeasure, then reason may be made to serve the interests of a will that is preoccupied with the satfaction of a natural inclination. Once again we have evidence of Kant's rejection of natural inclination on the ground that it obstructs the determination of the will by reason and moral law.

As we have seen, Kant in the "Analytic" is concerned to emphasise the importance of reason and moral law, and to protect those principles from any empirical influence. The most striking example of the change of emphasis (from the immanent principle of the good or autonomous will, principle (b) in the "Foundations", to the transcendent moral law, principle (a) in the "Critique of Practical Reason"), is provided by a comparison of the key passage in the "Foundations" (IV.432,90,supra p.36), with the following passage in the "Analytic", in which Kant explains the mistake made by philosophers in seeking a supreme principle of morality. -"Denn sie suchten einen Gegenstand des Willens auf, um ihn zur Materie und dem Grunde eines Gesetzes zu machen (welches alsdann nicht unmittelbar, sondern vermittelst jenes an das Gefühl der Lust oder Unlust gebrachten Gegenstandes der Bestimmungsgrund des Willens sein sollte),anstatt daß sie zuerst nach einem Gesetze hätten forschen sollen, das a priori und unmittelbar den Willen und diesem gemäß allererst den Gegenstand bestimmte. Nun mochten sie diesen Gegenstand der Lust, der den obersten Begriff des Guten abgeben sollte, in der Glückseligkeit, in der Vollkommenheit, im moralischen Gefühle, oder im Willen Gottes setzen, so war ihr Grundsatz allemal Heteronomie, sie mußten unvermeidlich auf empirische Bedingungen zu einem moralischen Gesetze stoßen; weil sie ihren Gegenstand, als unmittelbaren Bestimmungsgrund des Willens, nur nach seinem unmittelbaren Verhalten zum Gefühl, welches allemal empirisch ist, gut oder böse nennen konnten. Nur ein formales Gesetz, d.i. ein solches, welches der Vernunft nichts weiter als die Form ihrer allgemeinen Gesetzgebung zur obersten Bedingung der Maximen vorschreibt, kann a priori ein Bestimmungsgrund der praktischen Vernunft sein."

In this passage (V.64,172) Kant criticises the philosophers of earlier times because, in attempting to discover a supreme principle of morality, they "sought an object of the will, in order to make it the material and foundation of a law (which was then to be the ground of the determination of the will, not immediately, but by means of that object in relation to the feeling of pleasure or displeasure), instead of first looking about, as they should have

done, for a law that determined the will a priori
and immediately, and so only then determined the object in accordance with the will. Now whether they
identified this object of pleasure, which was to
supply the supreme principle of the good, in happiness, in perfection, in moral feeling, or in the
will of God, their principle was always heteronomy:
they could not avoid discovering empirical conditions of any such moral law, since they could call
their object good or bad, as the immediate ground of
determination of the will, only according to its
immediate relation to feeling, which is always empirical. Only a formal law, i.e. a law which lays
down for reason nothing more than the form of its
universal legislation as a supreme condition of maxims, can be a priori a ground of determination of
practical reason".

In both passages Kant looks back at the attempts of earlier philosophers to discover a principle of morality, and in both passages he complains
that the principle which they discovered was heteronomy. But there the parallel ends. In IV.432f.90 his
complaint is that an unsuccessful attempt was made
to impose on men certain absolute laws, which they
could be induced to accept only by offering them
certain adventitious "interests". These inducements,
particularly the "constraint" ("Zwang") which was
imposed on the will in an attempt to make it comply
with an absolute law, represented a heteronomous influence, because the will was to be made to obey the
law, not for the sake of the law, but for the sake
of the. inducement. In this case the principle of
autonomy that was infringed was the immanent or indwelling moral principle which we have referred to
as principle (b), as exemplified in the "Foundations" by the autonomous will – a principle capable,
not only of selecting a maxim which could serve as
a universal moral law, but also of devoting itself,
by virtue of its own inner impulse, to the fulfilment of that law.

In the corresponding passage in the "Critique

of Practical Reason" both the principle of heteronomy and that of autonomy are quite different. In
this case Kant complains that an attempt was made to
establish morality, not on a priori universal law,
but on some principle derived from the empirical
world, and capable of determining the will only by
means of heteronomous feeling, that is, some natural
inclination. In the second passage there is no spec-
ific reference to a principle of autonomy, though
the need for such a principle to counteract the heteronomous influence is clearly indicated. However,
Kant has already made it clear in this work that he
now has a different principle of autonomy in mind:
not the subjective indwelling principle (b), as exemplified by the good will in the "Foundations", but
the principle of transcendent reason, principle (a),
always ready to employ "constraint" against a will
that is apt to yield to natural inclinations.

We might well ask why Kant should have made
such a marked shift of emphasis in the "Critique of
Practical Reason". The change is partly explained by
the fact that he discusses different cases in the
two works. Kant's apparent austerity in the "Critique" is modified by the fact that autonomy is still
the basis of his argument. In the "Foundations" it
was the autonomy of a will which was true to its
moral function, but which had to employ the principle of autonomy even with respect to an authoritarian use of reason. In the "Critique" on the other
hand Kant discusses the case of a will which is not
truly moral, but which is even inclined to misuse
reason itself in its pursuit of its own selfish interests. In this case reason has to correct the
false "pathological" tendency in the will, and to
recall the will to its true function, that of supporting the autonomy of reason against the whole
world of nature. Moreover, we must not overlook the
significance of the fact that the "Critique" was
published one year before the outbreak of the French
Revolution in 1789. When Kant wrote the "Foundations" he had confidence in the moral forces which,

as he believed, were innate in the human will. But as the years passed, the forces that led to the Revolution became ever more questionable and menacing. It was only to be expected that the background of violence and reaction would be reflected in the work of the philosopher.

In the rest of this section on "The concept of an object of pure practical reason",there is further evidence of Kant's negative attitude to natural inclinations, so far as they relate to the morality of human conduct. It is here that he points out that such inclinations, "however they may be decked out", can only have a harmful effect. "If they are elevated" by empiricists "to the dignity of a supreme practical principle", they can only "degrade humanity" (71,179).

But the revisionists are tenacious, and in attempting to demonstrate that inclination is compatible with moral action, they have even tried to prove that, in the very formulation of the imperative of duty, the maxim at work in moral action arises normally from the cooperation of reason and inclination. For this purpose they appear to rely on a certain passage in the "Critique of Practical Reason" (67,176). -"So weiß man z.B. aus obiger Tafel...sogleich, wovon man in praktischen Erwägungen anfangen müsse: von den Maximen, die jeder auf seine Neigung gründet, den Vorschriften, die für eine Gattung vernünftiger Wesen, so fern sie in gewissen Neigungen übereinkommen, gelten, und endlich dem Gesetze, welches für alle unangesehen ihrer Neigungen gilt..."

There is a progression here, involving three categories. In the first category each individual bases his maxims on his inclinations; in the second the community applies certain agreed rules governing the ways in which certain inclinations may be expressed; and in the third category the moral law is applicable to all. In this last category inclinations have no relevance to moral law, which is applicable to all "irrespective of their inclination" ("unangesehen ihrer Neigungen").

Does the account of the three categories amount to "cooperation between reason and inclination", as certain critics appear to suggest? Only if we mix the categories, the reply must surely be. It is implied that in the first category maxims based by an individual on his subjective inclinations are of no moral value. In the second category rules governing the ways in which inclinations may be expressed in society, represent an attempt to maintain order in society, as distinct from moral laws. Only in the third category is the stage of universal moral law reached, and in this category inclinations play no part.

We now come to section three of the "Analytic", "Of the Motives of pure practical Reason" (71,180). Nowhere else is Kant's rejection of natural inclinations more absolute than in these pages. If the will is determined by a "feeling", in order that the latter may be a sufficient cause of the will, then the action will contain legality, but not morality (71, 180), because it will not be performed for the sake of the law. Kant's statement that it would be "hazardous" ("bedenklich") to allow "other motives", as well as the moral law, to influence the will, seems to have been taken by some critics as meaning that Kant does not absolutely rule out natural inclinations. But he immediately excludes that possibility, by declaring that the will must be determined by the law as a "free will", i.e. "not merely without the cooperation of sensuous impulses, but even by repudiating all such impulses, and by eliminating all inclinations, so far as they might be opposed to the law" (72,181). Kant is willing to concede that such natural inclinations as amount merely to a desire for happiness, and are not opposed to the law, can be accepted as "rational self-love" (72,181). But self-conceit or arrogance, opposed as it is to the law, is to be struck down by reason.

In discussing the will's "respect" for moral law, and in comparing Kant's treatment of this subject in the "Foundations" with his treatment of it in the second "Critique", critics usually pronounce the latter to be fuller and more satisfactory than the former. They do not seem to be fully aware that Kant's treatment of the subject is quite different in the two works. We have seen (supra p.13) that in a footnote added to IV.401,62, in the "Foundations", Kant brought out two aspects of the respect felt by the will for the moral law. In so far as the will is subject to the law, the respect that it feels has an analogy to "fear"; but in so far as the will imposes the law on itself, its respect for the law is analogous to "inclination" ("Neigung"). The importance of the idea of the autonomy of the will in the "Foundations" strongly suggests that it was mainly the analogy to "inclination" that Kant had in mind in referring in that work to the respect felt by the will for the law. In other words, "respect" in the "Foundations" exemplifies principle (b), a subjective disposition causing the will to act, not only according to the law, but also for the sake of the law.

In "The Critique of Practical Reason" on the other hand, in view of Kant's insistence on the need to eliminate natural inclinations opposed to the law, any respect felt by the will for the law must inevitably have an element of "fear" in it. Whereas in the passage on p.432,90 in the "Foundations" Kant deprecated a repressive imposition of the law, on the ground that it was opposed to the principle of the autonomy of the will (supra p.36), in the following passage from the "Critique" Kant associates the "respect" felt by the will, not only with a positive concept of the law as representing "intellectual causality" and "freedom", but more particularly with the law as representing a policy of repressing natural inclinations. -"Da dieses Gesetz aber doch etwas an sich Positives ist, nämlich die Form einer intellektuellen Kausalität,d.i. der Freiheit, so ist es, indem es im Gegensatze mit dem subjektiven Widerspiele, nämlich den Neigungen in uns, den Eigendünkel schwächt, zugleich ein Gegenstand der Achtung" (V.73,181). As we have seen, Kant is now concerned, less with the autonomy of the will, the indwelling moral principle (b), than with the autonomy of principle (a), reason and moral law. That is why he goes on to describe the respect that is felt for the moral law as the only feeling that is known to be 'a priori' ("dieses Gefühl ist das einzige, welches wir völlig a priori erkennen"). The will is now seen as an adjunct to reason and moral law, and it is the autonomy of the latter, the freedom of the noumenal world over against the forces of nature in the phenomenal world, that Kant has continually in mind. So he maintains that the respect felt by the will for the moral law originates in pure practical reason itself ("die Ursache der Bestimmung desselben liegt in der reinen praktischen Vernunft",75,183); and that respect for the law is not so much "a motive causing a person to act morally, as morality itself, regarded subjectively as a motive" (76,183).

We must compare this with Kant's treatment of "respect" in the "Foundations". Although, in that work, the will was in the first place described as feeling respect for the moral law, the will was itself later referred to as the proper object of respect (supra p.41); by which Kant meant that respect was to be accorded to the will itself. This shows the emphasis placed by Kant in the earlier work on principle (b), the indwelling subjective moral principle. In the Critique, on the other hand, so great is the emphasis on reason and moral law, principle (a), that Kant maintains that even the respect felt by the subjective will is really an effect of reason, an exemplification of the part played by principle (a) in determining the will.

At this point the tension between Kant's desire to keep his moral philosophy wholly intellectual, and his inability to exclude "feeling" altogether, becomes particularly apparent. It is something of a concession to empiricism that he is obliged to admit that respect is in fact a "moral feeling" (75,183); but he immediately goes on to dissociate respect from the kind of moral feeling espoused by the empiricists. In the case of respect for moral law, the original impulse comes from the law itself; and if the feeling of respect for moral law promotes the influence of the law on the will, this is not due to any subjective feeling (in favour of morality) preceding the original impulse of the law. -"Hier geht kein Gefühl im Subjekt vorher, das auf Moralität gestimmt wäre" (ibid).

It is perhaps in the following passage that the philosophy of Kant in the "Analytic" is most clearly explained. -"Das Bewußtsein einer freien Unterwerfung des Willens unter das Gesetz, doch als mit einem unvermeidlichen Zwange, der allen Neigungen, aber nur durch eigene Vernunft angetan wird, verbunden, ist nun die Achtung fürs Gesetz...Die Handlung, die nach diesem Gesetze, mit Ausschließung aller Bestimmungsgründe aus Neigung objektiv praktisch ist, heißt Pflicht, welche um dieser Ausschließung willen in ihrem Begriffe praktische Nötigung,d.i.Bestimmung zu Handlungen, so ungerne, wie sie auch geschehen mögen, enthält. Das Gefühl...enthält also,als Unterwerfung unter ein Gesetz, d.i. als Gebot (welches für das sinnlich affizierte Subjekt Zwang ankündigt), keine Lust, sondern so fern vielmehr Unlust an der Handlung in sich" (80,187f).

"The consciousness of a free subjection of the will to the law, but combined with unavoidable compulsion imposed on all inclinations, though only by one's own reason, is respect for the law...The action which according to this law (to the exclusion of all determination by inclination) is objectively practical, is called duty, which on account of this exclusion contains in its concept practical constraint, i.e. determination for actions, however unwillingly they may be carried out. The feeling...as subjection to a law, i.e a command (proclaiming compulsion for a sensuously affected subject), contains no pleasure, but rather displeasure in the action."

In this passage it appears that Kant wishes to reconcile the "constraint" ("Zwang" or "Nötigung"),

which he deems to be necessary in his moral philosophy, that is, the elimination of all determination
of the will by natural inclination, with the principle of autonomy or freedom. So he speaks of a "free
subjection" ("eine freie Unterwerfung") of the will
to the moral law, and points out that it is "only by
one's own reason" ("nur durch eigene Vernunft"),that
constraint or compulsion is imposed on all inclinations.

But it is not the autonomy of the will that Kant
is hoping to safeguard; for it is the will itself
that is subjected to the law ("eine Unterwerfung des
freien Willens"). Although it is the natural inclinations that are to be "excluded", it is implied that
the will, which has yielded to natural inclinations,
is also involved. Therefore, despite the reference
to the "free" will, it is not to the autonomy of the
will that Kant can appeal in this passage, but to
the autonomy of a "higher" principle, that of reason
itself. Whereas in the "Foundations" Kant spoke in-
timately and warmly of "our own will" (IV.440,97),
in the present passage he says that it is by one's
"own reason" ("durch eigene Vernunft") that natural
inclinations are constrained. Indeed, after the passage quoted, he further maintains that "since the
constraint is imposed merely by laws framed by one's
own reason, it also contains exaltation" ("Erheb-
ung"). The will is now seen in the wider context of
the "higher" principle of reason and moral law.After
the will has yielded to natural inclinations, its
autonomy has been forfeited; therefore the higher
autonomy of reason and moral law, as the supreme
principle of the noumenal world, must take the place
of the autonomy of the will. This seems to be implied by what Kant says.

In both passages Kant says that action must be
performed, not merely in conformity to the law, but
for the sake of the law; it must be not merely in
conformity to duty ("pflichtmäßig"), but must be
performed from a sense of duty ("aus Pflicht"). In
the "Critique" Kant speaks of the danger that the

agent might be satisfied by mere outward conformity
to the law (mere "legality"), by allowing the will
to be determined merely by "inclinations". -"Und
darauf beruht der Unterschied zwischen dem Bewußtsein, pflichtmäßig und aus Pflicht, d.i. aus Achtung
fürs Gesetz, gehandelt zu haben, davon das erstere
(die Legalität) auch möglich ist, wenn Neigungen
bloß die Bestimmungsgründe des Willens gewesen
wären, das zweite aber (die Moralität), der moralische Wert, lediglich darin gesetzt werden muß, daß
die Handlung aus Pflicht, d.i. bloß um des Gesetzes
willen, geschehe" (V.81,188). Thus in the "Critique"
it is natural inclination that represents the danger
of heteronomy.

But in the passage from the "Foundations" (IV.
432,90) Kant maintained that if the moral law were
reinforced by constraint (in excluding natural inclinations), the ensuing action could never be regarded as "unconditionally" ("unbedingt") good,since
the will would be acting, not out of respect for the
moral law itself, but in response to the constraint
associated with the moral law. So Kant's argument in
the "Foundations" seems to refute his very different
argument in the "Critique". In the latter work respect for the law arises, not from a feeling analogous to "Neigung" (in the sense of a certain affinity that the will feels with the moral law), but
from "fear or at least concern with respect to the
danger of transgressing against the law" ("Achtung
fürs Gesetz, welche mit Furcht oder wenigstens Be-
sorgnis vor Übertretung verbunden ist",81,189). Thus
Kant's reference to "respect" for the law (in the
footnote to IV.401,62), serves to mark the distinction between his very different views concerning
"respect" in the two works: respect for the law felt
by a will conscious of a certain affinity with the
law (in the "Foundations"), and "respect" in the
sense of fear of the law (in the "Critique"). But as
we have said, the latter type of respect is rejected
in the "Foundations", because to act according to
the law, and yet from fear of the constraint of the

law, fails to satisfy the requirement that moral action must be "unconditional", which it cannot be, if it is performed, not for the sake of the law, but for fear of the "constraint" associated with the law.

Kant has certainly not abandoned the compatibility that exists in the "Foundations" between the "good will" and the moral law, a compatibility that is reflected in the idea of the autonomy of the will. All that he does is to reject the idea that we could ever cultivate what he calls a "holy" will, by establishing an unfailing agreement of the will with the pure moral law, by virtue of which agreement the ability to act for the sake of the law would become second nature to the will.

"Gleich als ob wir es dahin jemals bringen könnten,daß ohne Achtung fürs Gesetz...wir...gleichsam durch eine uns zur Natur gewordene, niemals zu verrückende Übereinstimmung des Willens mit dem reinen Sittengesetze...jemals in den Besitz einer Heiligkeit des Willens kommen könnten" (V.81,189). In the opinion of Kant in his present austere mood, to feel love and sympathy for mankind is to put ourselves as "volunteers" above the idea of duty (82,189). Kant has not altogether forgotten the idea of the autonomy of the will, but now his main concern is with "duty", "constraint" and "reverence" ("Ehrfurcht", a word which includes "fear"). It is true, he agrees, that we are "lawmaking members of a free kingdom of morality; but nevertheless we remain at the same time subjects of this kingdom, not the supreme head" (ibid). So Kant indicates in this work that the autonomous will, principle (b), is to be regarded as subordinate to the "higher" autonomy of reason and moral law, principle (a). Our will stands under the discipline of reason ("Wir stehen unter einer Disziplin der Vernunft", ibid), and it is for the will to assist reason in enforcing the law by resisting the unruly forces of nature.

Kant's adverse references to voluntarism follow close on the heels of the passage in which he argues that action which is carried out from the motive of "respect" for moral law can scarcely be performed without a certain "unwillingness" ("Bestimmung zu Handlungen, so ungerne, wie sie auch geschehen mögen",80,187), or perhaps even a certain displeasure ("keine Lust, sondern so fern vielmehr Unlust an der Handlung",80,188); the unwillingness or displeasure which result from the need to sacrifice natural inclinations. So we are asked to accept the rather strange conclusion that actions which are carried out in the approved Kantian manner, that is, "for the sake of the law", must be performed reluctantly; whereas actions which are carried out with all the dedication of moral feeling, or as we might say, from natural sympathy, by people to whom it has become second nature to suit their actions to the pure moral law, are to be rejected on the ground that they have not been carried out from a sense of duty. "Unwillingness" in this context refers to the unwillingness of the agent to forgo the satisfaction of a natural inclination, for the sake of the obedience which he owes to a moral law.

It is instructive to note how Kant deals with the following biblical commandment.

"Liebe Gott über alles und deinen Nächsten als dich selbst" (83,189).

"Love God above all and your fellow being as yourself."

It is not surprising that Kant, as a rationalist, should wish to eliminate the word "love"; nor is it surprising, in view of the important part that the moral law plays in his moral philosophy, that he should wish to substitute for the word "love" the words "commandments" and "duty".

"Gott lieben, heißt in dieser Bedeutung, seine Gebote gerne tun; den Nächsten lieben, heißt, alle Pflicht gegen ihn gerne ausüben" (83,190).

"In this sense, to love God means to carry out his commandments willingly; to love one's fellow human being means to perform every duty towards him willingly."

So Kant has arrived at the rationalistically satisfying idea of "carrying out a commandment" or "performing a duty". In fact he has transformed the biblical message into a rational principle, indeed principle (a). But at this point a strange and an interesting thing appears to have happened. Although Kant probably considered the word "gerne" ("willingly") appropriate as a means of eliminating the idea of "love" (a word which, despite its biblical meaning of "charity", may have seemed suggestive of a natural inclination), once the word "willingly" was in his text, it seems to have assumed a different complexion. To carry out God's commandments willingly, to perform one's duty gladly - what is that but to act from the right moral disposition in carrying out the moral law, in fact to act in the spirit of principle (b), while acting on principle (a)? So Kant carries over from the "Foundations" to the "Critique" the idea of the agreement or compatibility between the subjective moral disposition and the objective moral law produced by reason.

But now Kant modifies this idea, by saying that the agreement between the two principles can never be complete. Since people can never entirely free themselves from desires and inclinations which are opposed to the law, it follows that at the present stage in their moral development, they cannot yet attain the required standard in their moral disposition (84,191). The commandment referred to represents the moral disposition in all its perfection, a scarcely attainable ideal of holiness, for which we should nevertheless strive through infinite time.

"Jenes Gesetz aller Gesetze stellt also, wie alle moralische Vorschrift des Evangelii, die sittliche Gesinnung in ihrer ganzen Vollkommenheit dar, so wie sie als ein Ideal der Heiligkeit von keinem Geschöpfe erreichbar, dennoch das Urbild ist, welchem wir uns zu nähern und in einem ununterbrochenen, aber unendlichen Progressus gleich zu werden streben sollen" (83,190).

In the meantime we must act in accordance with

our "duty". In view of the morally imperfect state
of man, our moral condition can at best be one of
"virtue" ("Tugend"), a principle described by Kant
in terms of a continual "Kampf" or "struggle" with
natural inclinations. This struggle, which is con-
stantly being fought out in each person, is in stark
contrast to the over-optimistic belief in a will
supposedly endowed with a morally pure disposition.

"Sein moralischer Zustand...ist Tugend, d.i.
moralische Gesinnung im Kampfe, und nicht Heiligkeit
im vermeintlichen Besitze einer völligen Reinigkeit
der Gesinnungen des Willens" (84,191).

In one sense Kant has downgraded the inner subjective moral disposition, by stressing the morally
imperfect disposition of man. Therefore the will,
contending with unruly inclinations and dangerous
passions, must turn for support to the moral law itself, formulated by reason. Nevertheless,even though
man cannot yet reach the stage at which the subjective disposition coincides with objective moral law,
his ultimate purpose must be to bring about just
such an agreement between the two principles. Only
if such an ideal were to be realised, would morality
"cease to be virtue" (i.e. morality always having to
contend with natural inclinations), because instead
of depending on a separate rational-moral principle,
it would itself pass over into "holiness" ("Moralität, die nun subjektiv in Heiligkeit überginge,würde
aufhören, Tugend zu sein",84,191). Therefore, in so
far as Kant looks forward to such an ideal state of
"holiness", he has in fact upgraded the subjective
moral disposition. But man's longing for such an
ideal moral consummation must not be confused with
the "moral fanaticism" ("moralische Schwärmerei")
which some writers seek to spread,nor with the ideas
of "sentimental educationists" (86,192).

The apostrophe which Kant addresses to "Duty"
("Duty! Sublime, great name...") epitomizes the most
obvious of Kant's philosophic positions in the present work. -"Pflicht! du erhabener, großer Name, der
du...bloß ein Gesetz aufstellst, welches von selbst

im Gemüte Eingang findet und doch sich selbst wider
Willen Verehrung (wenn gleich nicht immer Befolgung)
erwirbt, vor dem alle Neigungen verstummen, wenn sie
gleich insgeheim ihm entgegen wirken..." (86,193).

"Duty! Sublime, great name, you who...merely
establish a law, which of itself enters the mind,
gaining for itself a certain involuntary reverence
(though not always compliance), before which all inclinations are reduced to silence, even though they
secretly work against it..."

So, in this key passage, Kant again stresses
the incompatibility between natural inclinations and
the duty of obeying the moral law set up by reason.
It is an incompatibility which he continues to emphasise when he requires Duty to inform him of its
"noble ancestry", which as he says, "proudly repudiates all connection with inclinations" ("Wo findet
man die Wurzel deiner edlen Abkunft, welche alle
Verwandtschaft mit Neigungen stolz ausschlägt?").

Kant replies on behalf of Duty by describing
its ancestry negatively, that is, in terms of whatever is distinct from the natural order. It is nothing less than what "raises man (as a part of the
sensuous world) above himself" ("Es kann nichts Min-
deres sein, als was den Menschen über sich selbst
(als einen Teil der Sinnenwelt) erhebt", ibid). When
at last Kant refers to man's higher self in more
positive terms, that is, in terms of man's "person-
ality and freedom", and of the "pure practical laws
produced by his own reason", he still finds it necessary to remind us that this higher self represents
"independence from the mechanism of the whole of
nature". -"Es ist nichts anders als die Persönlichkeit, d.i. die Freiheit und Unabhängigkeit von dem
Mechanism der ganzen Natur, doch zugleich als ein
Vermögen eines Wesens betrachtet, welches eigentüm-
lichen, nämlich von seiner eigenen Vernunft gegeben-
en, reinen praktischen Gesetzen...unterworfen ist."

At this point, as indeed throughout the "Analytic", Kant emphasises reason and the moral law produced by reason. Thus he reintroduces the idea of

autonomy. But now, instead of placing the emphasis
on the autonomy of the will,as in the "Foundations",
he subordinates the latter to the autonomy of reason. He also uses the occasion to take up again the
idea of man as an end in himself. Everything else in
the whole of creation, except man, can be used as a
means to an end. Only man, as a rational being, is
an end in himself. "For he is the subject of the
moral law, which is holy, by virtue of the autonomy
of his freedom." -"Er ist nämlich das Subjekt des
moralischen Gesetzes, welches heilig ist, vermöge
der Autonomie seiner Freiheit" (87,193).

So Kant, combining the principle of autonomy
with that of man as an end in himself, indicates the
way in which we should proceed if we wished to treat
another person in accordance with those two principles. -"Eben um dieser willen ist jeder Wille,selbst
jeder Person ihr eigener, auf sie selbst gerichteter
Wille auf die Bedingung der Einstimmung mit der
Autonomie des vernünftigen Wesens eingeschränkt, es
nämlich keiner Absicht zu unterwerfen, die nicht
nach einem Gesetze, welches aus dem Willen des
leidenden Subjekts selbst entspringen könnte, möglich ist; also dieses niemals bloß als Mittel, sondern zugleich selbst als Zweck zu gebrauchen."

"Every will, i.e. in the case of each person,
his own will, directed to himself, is limited to the
condition that it must agree with the autonomy of
the rational being, that is, to subject it to no
purpose not possible according to a law which might
arise from the will of the affected subject itself;
and thus to use the latter never merely as a means,
but at the same time as itself a purpose" (87,193f).

In this passage Kant is thinking of two persons: the first person who is considering how best
he should treat a second person; and the second person, who (because he will be affected by the treatment),is called the "passive" subject. It is assumed
that both persons are rational beings. The treatment
that should be meted out to the second person,should
agree with a law which he himself might well have
produced autonomously by his own will.

At the beginning of the section entitled "The critical elucidation of the analytic of pure practical reason" (89,195), we have an interesting illustration of Kant's tendency to think of moral conduct in terms of excluding natural inclination. In this case he does so by making use of a chemical analogy, in discussing the conduct of a person who is tempted to tell a lie for his own advantage. Just as an analytical chemist, with a solution of lime in muriatic acid, adds an alkali, thus separating out the acid from the lime, and causing it to unite with the alkali; just so does an otherwise honourable man, tempted to tell a lie, pause to consider the moral law. At once his practical reason spurns the advantage he might have gained by lying; and henceforth, with his reason firmly attached to moral law, he is cured of his wrongdoing (92,199).

In a comment on this illustration of the necessity of separating out all natural inclination (in this case self-interest), to ensure truly moral action, Kant makes it clear that he is not implying that we need give up all hope of happiness; indeed, in certain circumstances, it may even be one's duty to consider one's happiness. This is the kind of passage which the revisionists are inclined to misuse, by suggesting that Kant is not after all so firmly committed to excluding natural inclination from his moral philosophy, as he is sometimes supposed to be. What Kant says is that there is no need to sacrifice our happiness in all circumstances, but only when "it is a question of duty" ("sondern nur, sobald von Pflicht die Rede ist",93,199). The word "only" in this passage in fact refers to Kant's main concern, i.e. "duty" or moral conduct. So he still makes it quite clear that we should not allow the thought of our happiness to come between us and our duty. Again, when Kant says that it may sometimes be our duty to consider our own happiness, he makes it clear that this is because happiness may indirectly be the means whereby we are enabled to do our duty, e.g. in the case of any skill we may have, our

health, or our financial resources; whereas unhappiness, for instance as a result of poverty, may prevent us from doing our duty. So here Kant is regard-
ing happiness, resulting from the satisfaction of
our natural inclinations, as serving indirectly as
a means to an end, the performance of our duty. But
if on the other hand the thought of happiness tends
to distract us from attending to our duty, this is
a very different situation. In this case Kant is
completely opposed to the belief that, when the will
is engaged in making a moral decision, it should be
motivated in any way by the thought of happiness.
-"Da nun alle Bestimmungsgründe des Willens außer
dem einzigen reinen praktischen Vernunftgesetze (dem
moralischen) insgesammt empirisch sind, als solche
also zum Glückseligkeitsprinzip gehören, so müssen
sie insgesammt vom obersten sittlichen Grundsatze
abgesondert und ihm nie als Bedingung einverleibt
werden" (93,199).

"As all factors determining the will, apart
from the one pure practical (and moral) law of reason, are entirely empirical, and as such belong to
the principle of happiness, they must all be separated out from the supreme moral principle, and must
never be incorporated with it as a condition."

Kant's message is clear and unambiguous. Natural
inclinations, by the satisfaction of which people
seek to gain happiness, must be "abgesondert", that
is, separated out from moral law. In fact we have
previously referred (supra p.13) to a similar passage in the "Foundations" (IV.400,61), containing a
statement that an action from duty must completely
"separate out" ("absondern") the influence of inclination.

Kant has already introduced the distinction between the world of "appearances" and that of "things
in themselves" (in the earlier section "Concerning
the right of pure reason to an extension of its
practical use not possible to it in its speculative
use", V.50,160). Now, in the "Critical elucidation
of the Analytic of pure practical reason", he considers the implications of this distinction. In the

first place, he is not disposed to underestimate the advantage to be gained by the concept of a world of "noumena" or "things in themselves". It is nothing less than the "glorious revelation, granted to us through pure practical reason by means of moral law ...of an intelligible world brought about by the transcendent concept of freedom" (V.94,200). This great gain would be lost if we were to accept the false teaching of empiricists, that freedom is merely psychological or comparative, instead of transcendental and absolute" (97,203). According to that theory, our "freedom" would be no better than that of a turnspit, which needs to be wound up, before it can perform its movements (ibid). On the other hand, a person who is conscious of himself as a "thing-in-himself" or a "noumenon", is convinced that he is "determinable by laws which he gives himself by virtue of his reason" (ibid). In this way it is mainly by an appeal to our consciousness, to the way in which we feel about ourselves, as well as to the principle of autonomy, that Kant gives greater reality to the idea of the noumenon as distinct from the phenomenon."From this point of view, it can truly be said of every immoral action that a person has committed (even though as a phenomenon it was sufficiently determined, and to that extent unavoidably necessary) that he could have avoided it; for that action, together with all the past events that determined it, belonged to a single phenomenon of his character, which he creates for himself; and therefore, as a cause independent of all sensuous existence, he attributes to himself the causality of those phenomena" (ibid).

So Kant insists that we (as noumena), so to speak, create our own character, even though our actions (as phenomena) seem to follow one from another in a determined series. Furthermore, he appeals very convincingly to our experience of the way in which our conscience works. However hard we may attempt, when we recall some misdeed that we committed long ago, to excuse ourselves by maintaining

that we were, so to speak, "carried along by the
stream of natural necessity" ("vom Strom der Natur-
notwendigkeit fortgerissen",98,204), the repentance
that we nevertheless feel, even though it can have
no practical effect, still testifies to the judgment
of our reason in condemning the misdeed, despite any
appeal to "natural necessity". Kant also quotes the
case of a person who shows such an early tendency to
wrongdoing, a tendency which persists into his years
of manhood, that an observer is inclined to write
him off as an inveterate and incorrigible villain,
owing to the evil qualities with which nature has
endowed him. Yet we still continue to regard him as
responsible for his actions, since his uniformly
wicked conduct is "the consequence of his voluntarily adopted evil and persistent principles" ("die
Folge der freiwillig bösen und unwandelbaren Grundsätze",100,205).

Kant now refers to a danger that "threatens
freedom with its complete destruction". If one ac-
cepts that God is the cause of everything that exists, one must also concede that the actions of men
must be determined by something quite beyond their
control, namely, by the causality of an exalted being on whom they are wholly dependent (100,206). But
Kant, in introducing this difficulty, at the same
time suggests the means whereby the danger to freedom may be removed. "If the actions of men, and the
way in which they are determined in time, were not
merely determinations of those actions as phenomena,
but as things-in-themselves, freedom could not be
saved."

"Wären die Handlungen des Menschen, so wie sie
zu seinen Bestimmungen in der Zeit gehören, nicht
bloße Bestimmungen desselben als Erscheinung,sondern
als Dinges an sich selbst, so würde die Freiheit
nicht zu retten sein" (101,206).

Kant proceeds to demonstrate that God cannot
have determined human actions in that way,for otherwise the agents could not be human beings as we understand them to be, i.e. free human beings. "Man

would be a marionette, or an automaton devised by Vaucanson, constructed and wound up by a supreme technical master. Self-consciousness would indeed make it a "thinking" automaton, in which however the consciousness of its spontaneity, if it were regarded as freedom, would be merely deceptive, since only in a comparative sense would it deserve to be called that; because the proximate determining causes of its movement, and a long series of their determining causes would indeed be internal, but the ultimate and highest of them would nevertheless be in the hands of another being" (101,206).

Furthermore, if we assumed that God determined our actions in this way, not only would our consciousness of freedom be illusory, but also God himself would be subject to time and space, which would contradict our belief in his infinity and independence (101,207). Kant concludes that the concept of God's act of creation applies, not to physical existence, or to causality, but only to things-in-themselves or noumena (102,207).

"Just as it would be a contradiction to say that God is a creator of appearances (phenomena), so it is also a contradiction to say that he as creator is the cause of actions in the physical world, as phenomena, even though he is the cause of the existence of the agents, as noumena. If it is possible...to maintain the principle of freedom without prejudice to the natural mechanism of actions as phenomena, so the fact that the agents have been created, cannot make the slightest difference, because creation concerns their intelligible, but not their sensible existence, and therefore cannot be regarded as the determining principle of phenomena; though the result would be very different, if the creatures of this world existed as things-in-themselves in time, because in that case the creator of substantial being would at the same time be the author of the whole mechanistic nature of this substance" (102,208).

We now come to the second part of the "Critique of Practical Reason", the "Dialectic".

The "Dialectic of pure practical Reason" was in a sense necessitated by the effect on Kant's moral philosophy of the "Transcendental Dialectic" in the "Critique of Pure Reason". Here his aim was the speculative one of demonstrating that the world perceived by the mind (the world of "appearances") is not simply the objective world ("out there"), but is so to speak conditioned by what the mind itself contributes to the act of perception, the categories of space and time for instance, or the a priori ideas of pure mathematics, or the "necessity" of what we regard as causality in the world of "appearances". Thus Kant was justified in claiming that he had overcome the "antinomies" by uniting mind and matter, and by bringing about the kind of "synthesis" which is typical of the form of the Dialectic.

But Kant also makes it clear that this "Copernican" revolution which he has carried out has important implications, not only for speculative reason, but also for moral philosophy. By rescuing us from the world of phenomena, the world of mechanistic causality, he also transports us to a "noumenal" world no longer subject to determinism. Kant could scarcely have given clearer expression to the moral advantages of separating the noumenal world from that of "appearances", than he does in the following passage in the "Critique of Pure Reason". –"That the world should have a beginning, that my thinking self should be simple and therefore imperishable in nature, that in its voluntary actions it should be free and raised above natural necessity, and finally that the whole order of things which make up the world should derive from an original being, from whom everything obtains its unity and its purposive combination – all these things are so many foundation-stones of morality and religion" (III.324).

On the other hand Kant has had to pay a high price for his charmed noumenal world, his haven of freedom and morality. It might be maintained that, having for speculative purposes created a synthesis of mind and matter, he has, for practical and moral

purposes, created a division between the world of
moral freedom and that of nature; that he has de-
prived the natural world of its moral resources, and
abandoned it to its "Naturmechanism", its contingency and its determinism.

There are disadvantages in attempting to with-
draw to a noumenal world, turning one's back on the
despised world of nature; for one thing it is not
even possible. Even in his apostrophe to Duty, that
supreme principle of the noumenal world, Kant reminds us that man, whether he likes it or not, belongs to both worlds ("der Mensch, als zu beiden
Welten gehörig",87,193). The moral principle from
which one acts may be derived from the noumenal
world, but the effects are seen in the empirical
world; and it is always with a view to determining
the will of man as a creature of the natural world
that moral laws are formulated.

However hard Kant has striven to uphold the
principle of transcendent reason, and to ward off
any unwanted empirical influence, he has also felt
the need to bridge the gulf between the rational-
moral world and the empirical world. The natural inclinations, against which he must remain on guard,
must not be allowed to stand in the way of this second aim.

But if Kant's present purpose is to bring about
a synthesis between nature and morality, he makes it
clear that he has no intention of abandoning his
negative attitude to the part played by natural inclinations in morality. In one passage of the "Dialectic" he refers appreciatively to what might at
first appear to be a certain "aesthetic" side of human nature, a certain sensuous "feeling", but on the
other hand he maintains that it is an illusion to
think of this aesthetic quality in such empirical
terms. -"Es ist etwas sehr Erhabenes in der menschlichen Natur, unmittelbar durch ein reines Vernunft-
gesetz zu Handlungen bestimmt zu werden, und sogar
die Täuschung, das Subjektive dieser intellektuellen
Bestimmbarkeit des Willens für etwas Ästhetisches

und Wirkung eines besondern sinnlichen Gefühls (denn ein intellektuelles wäre ein Widerspruch) zu halten" (117,221). Even though Kant refers to the importance of cultivating such "aesthetic" feeling, he again makes it clear that it is to be regarded as an "effect" of reason. –"Es ist auch von großer Wichtigkeit, auf diese Eigenschaft unserer Persönlichkeit aufmerksam zu machen, und die Wirkung der Vernunft auf dieses Gefühl bestmöglichst zu kultivieren."

Although Kant concedes that an "inclination to duty" may facilitate the effectiveness of moral maxims, he then adds that such an inclination cannot actually produce a moral maxim. –"Selbst eine Neigung zum Pflichtmäßigen (z.B. zur Wohltätigkeit) kann zwar die Wirksamkeit der moralischen Maximen sehr erleichtern, aber keine hervorbringen" (118,222).

Indeed in the rest of the passage Kant makes his usual criticism of natural inclination, from a moral point of view. "Inclination is blind and servile, whether it is of the good variety or not... Even a feeling of pity, and soft-hearted sympathy, if it precedes the thought of duty, and becomes the determining factor, is irksome to right-thinking people" (ibid). In view of the fact that Kant regards natural inclinations as merely "instinctive" or "mechanistic", it is difficult to see how such an inclination would be able, in his moral philosophy, to cooperate with reason and moral law. Surely, only if Kant were to repudiate his rejection of pure nature, only if he were to cease to think of nature in terms of "instincts", could we believe that the two worlds, the empirical world of nature, and the world of the rational-moral law, might cease to be what they have usually been in his moral philosophy, two worlds existing for ever apart from each other.

Fortunately Kant has at his disposal another principle which, instead of undermining moral law (as in his opinion natural inclinations tend to do), serves rather to support it. This other principle is the second of the two archetypal moral principles, principle (b), a subjective immanent principle predisposing a person to act in the spirit of the law.

It was represented in the "Foundations", firstly by
the "good" will, whose function it was to support
universal moral law, and secondly by the "autonomous" will, whose function seemed at times to go beyond the duty of supporting moral law. It was the
"Gesinnung", the moral "disposition", another exemplification of principle (b), which played a key
part in the universal lawgiving of rational beings
(in the "Foundations",IV.435f,supra 45f); and it is
the moral disposition which likewise plays the leading rôle in the "Dialectic".

The part which the "Gesinnung" is capable of
playing is already foreshadowed in the "Analytic",
where it is contrasted with the kind of action which
sometimes results from a natural inclination, an
action which, quite by chance, might possibly agree
with a moral law, but which was not performed for
the sake of the law (V.71,LWB.180). The distinction
between an action that is carried out for the sake
of moral law, and one that is merely performed "in
conformity" to the law, is an important one, because
it implies the difference between an agent who is
inwardly committed to morality, and an agent who has
no such inner commitment, but who might merely be
concerned to see that his conduct conforms outwardly
to moral law (which outward conformity is referred
to by Kant as "legality" in contradistinction to
"morality").

It is precisely an inner commitment that is implied by Kant's concept of the moral "disposition"
(the "Gesinnung"). We are told for instance that the
motive of the will must always be the moral law,
"unless the action is to fulfil merely the letter of
the law, without the spirit of it". To this Kant
adds the following footnote. "Man kann von jeder gesetzmäßigen Handlung, die doch nicht um des Gesetzes
willen geschehen ist, sagen: sie sei bloß dem Buch-
staben, aber nicht dem Geiste (der Gesinnung) nach
moralisch gut" (72,180).

"Of every action that is carried out in conformity to the law, but not for the sake of the law, it

can be said that it is morally good merely according to the letter, but not according to the spirit (the disposition)".

It might be regarded as somewhat surprising that in a work like Kant's "Critique of Practical Reason", distinguished as it is by the pre-eminent part played by reason and moral law, the "Gesinnung" or disposition should play a scarcely less important part. But this is explained by the fact that the "Gesinnung" is both a subjective moral disposition, and at the same time a principle whose whole purpose is to bring about action in the very spirit of objective moral law. Far from acting as a rival principle, the disposition is itself dedicated to the fulfilment of the law.

Kant is concerned to distinguish the moral disposition (which plays a key rôle in determining the will to act morally) from a natural inclination or a sensuous feeling. -"Hier geht kein Gefühl im Subjekt vorher, das auf Moralität gestimmt wäre. Denn das ist unmöglich, weil alles Gefühl sinnlich ist; die Triebfeder der sittlichen Gesinnung aber muß von aller sinnlichen Bedingung frei sein" (75,183).

"Here there is no prior feeling in the subject that might tend to morality, because all feeling is sensuous; but the motive of the moral disposition must be free from all sensuous influence."

In other words, although the moral "Gesinnung", as a subjective principle, has a certain analogy with a natural feeling such as sympathy, it is nonetheless distinct from such a natural feeling. With respect to the dividing line that separates the natural order from the intelligible world, it lies on the latter side, together with reason and moral law.

As compared with Kant's treatment of the "Gesinnung", his account of the concept of "Achtung" ("respect") is more complicated, since it varies between his statement in the "Foundations" that the will is the proper object of respect, to his assertion in the "Critique" that respect is "morality itself", i.e. the rational-moral principle regarded subjectively as a motive (supra pp.61-64).

Respect for moral law, as it is represented in the "Analytic", has an "intellectual" basis, and although it is a "feeling", it is unique in the sense that it is the only feeling that can be apprehended "a priori". -"Also ist Achtung fürs moralische Gesetz ein Gefühl, welches durch einen intellektuellen Grund gewirkt wird, und dieses Gefühl ist das einzige, welches wir völlig a priori erkennen"(73,181).

By attributing to "respect" a certain intellectual understanding, Kant is able to suggest that this principle is able to appreciate the work of the moral law in upholding freedom by suppressing man's natural inclinations. -"Da dieses Gesetz aber doch an sich etwas Positives ist, nämlich die Form einer intellektuellen Kausalität, d.i. der Freiheit, so ist es, indem es im Gegensatze mit dem subjektiven Widerspiele, nämlich den Neigungen in uns, den Eigendünkel schwächt, zugleich ein Gegenstand der Achtung" (73,181).

In the first section of the "Dialectic" Kant introduces his idea of the Summum Bonum, the Highest Good, by attributing to reason the following aims.

"As pure practical reason it likewise seeks the Unconditional for what is practically conditional (resting on inclinations and natural needs); and not as the determining principle of the will, but even when this is already given (in the moral law), it seeks the unconditional totality of the object of pure practical reason under the name of the Highest Good (the Summum Bonum)" (108,212).

"Sie sucht als reine praktische Vernunft zu dem praktisch Bedingten (was auf Neigungen und Naturbedürfnis beruht) ebenfalls das Unbedingte, und zwar nicht als Bestimmungsgrund des Willens, sondern, wenn dieser auch (im moralischen Gesetze) gegeben worden, die unbedingte Totalität des Gegenstandes der reinen praktischen Vernunft, unter dem Namen des höchsten Guts."

In the "Analytic" Kant was much concerned with the "unconditional" character of moral law as given by reason, and with the function of reason (in the

interest of morality) in determining the will by
means of moral law, in such a way as to control and
if necessary to repress the conditional "inclinations and natural needs" of man. But now, in the
"Dialectic", to judge by the terms in which he introduces the "Summum Bonum", it appears that he is
less interested in the task of controlling natural
inclinations by moral law, than in the need to mod-
ify their conditional character. When Kant refers to
the "Summum Bonum" as the "unconditional totality of
the object of pure practical reason", he appears to
be referring to a future ideal state of man in which
not only would the human will be determined unconditionally by moral law, but also the totality of his
self would be liberated from the "conditional" character of his natural inclinations, subject as these
are to natural necessity. In other words, under the
concept of the "Summum Bonum", Kant envisages a human state in which the "unconditional" character of
moral law would apply also to man as a member of the
natural order. The "Summum Bonum" is both an unconditional moral concept like that of moral law, and
also an all-embracing principle uniting the rational
world with the empirical world in a dialectical synthesis.

How then can man liberate himself from the conditional character of his natural inclinations?
"Happiness", which is to be an essential part of the
"Summum Bonum", has hitherto meant the satisfaction
of man's innate inclinations, the fulfilment of his
desires; yet it is precisely through these inclinations and desires that man has subjected himself to
certain "conditions" which must be met if he is to
fulfil his desire for happiness. Unlike moral laws,
which determine, in an absolute sense, what a certain person must do, natural inclinations indicate
what he must do as a condition which he must fulfil
in order to satisfy his desire. Therefore, if the
life of man, not only as a moral being "per se", but
also as a member of the natural order, is to be made
"unconditional" in its "totality", the basis of his

happiness must be changed: it must be based no longer on the satisfaction of his desires, but on the
fulfilment of the moral law.

Hitherto the "happiness principle", the need to
satisfy one's inclinations, has conflicted with the
true moral character of man. When natural inclination affects the will, it introduces heteronomy, and
challenges the will's autonomy, its ability to determine itself by means of the moral law supplied by
its own reason; but if virtue is purchased by sacri-
ficing happiness, it will shine with all the greater
splendour. This has been Kant's position so far.

Now, however, in section two of the "Dialectic",
"Of the Dialectic of pure reason in determining the
concept of the Highest Good", the conflict between
morality and happiness is considerably modified. We
are at once struck by a new definition of virtue:
"die Würdigkeit glücklich zu sein", or "being worthy
of happiness" (110,215). Kant's more positive attitude to happiness in the "Dialectic" is explained as
follows. -"Denn der Glückseligkeit bedürftig, ihrer
auch würdig, dennoch aber derselben nicht teilhaftig
zu sein, kann mit dem vollkommenen Wollen eines vernünftigen Wesens, welches zugleich alle Gewalt hätte
...gar nicht zusammen bestehen."

"To need happiness, to be worthy of it, and yet
not to participate in it, cannot be consistent with
the perfect volition of a rational and at the same
time omnipotent being."

As already indicated by the new definition of
virtue, the happiness referred to in this passage
is obviously not to be identified with the satisfaction of man's natural inclinations. It is happiness
based on morality. Kant envisages "Glückseligkeit,
ganz genau in Proportion der Sittlichkeit...ausge-
teilt" ("Happiness distributed in exact proportion
to morality").

As Kant reminds us in this section, happiness
and morality are two quite distinct elements of the
Highest Good,which results from a synthesis of these
two elements (112,217). In discussing their relative

importance, Kant takes into consideration the views
of the Epicureans and the Stoics. To the former,
happiness was the essence of the Highest Good, and
virtue served simply as an entitlement to it. To the
Stoic on the other hand "happiness was already contained in the consciousness of his virtue" ("Das Gefühl der Glückseligkeit war dagegen nach dem Stoiker
schon im Bewußtsein seiner Tugend enthalten"). It is
clear that Kant's views are closer to those of the
Stoic than to those of the Epicurean. Virtue is the
"supreme condition...of all our claims to happiness"
("die oberste Bedingung...aller unserer Bewerbung um
Glückseligkeit",110,215). Virtue itself is not subject to any condition, but happiness "always presupposes moral conduct in conformity to the law as
its condition" ("jederzeit das moralische gesetzmäß-
ige Verhalten als Bedingung voraussetzt",111,215).

The logical steps by which Kant proceeds in the
Dialectic, leading to its conclusion in the concept
of the Highest Good, are clear enough. The "Antinomy
of Practical Reason" consists firstly of the thesis
that "the desire for happiness must be the motive
for maxims of virtue" (which is obviously a thesis
that is contrary to morality), and secondly of the
antithesis, which states that "the maxim of virtue
must be the efficient cause of happiness (113,217),
a proposition which must also be rejected on the
ground that it is impossible for events in the world
to correspond to the moral condition of the will.

There follows the section containing the "critical resolution of the antinomy of practical reason"
(114,218). As before the antinomy is resolved by
means of the distinction between the world of appearances and the noumenal world. "The first of the
two propositions, that the striving for happiness
gives a basis for a virtuous disposition ("einen
Grund tugendhafter Gesinnung") is absolutely false;
but the second,that a virtuous disposition ("Tugend-
gesinnung") necessarily produces happiness, is not
positively false, but only in so far as it is regarded as the form of causality in the sensible world".

Kant continues as follows. -"But as I am not only justified in thinking of my existence as a noumenon in the intelligible world, but also that in the moral law I even have a purely intellectual determining ground of my causality (in the sensible world), it is therefore not impossible that the morality of the disposition ("die Sittlichkeit der Gesinnung") has a necessary connection, if not directly, then indirectly (by means of an intelligible author of nature), as the cause of happiness in the sensible world" (114,218).

"So ist es nicht unmöglich, daß die Sittlichkeit der Gesinnung einen, wo nicht unmittelbaren, doch mittelbaren (vermittelst eines intelligibelen Urhebers der Natur) und zwar notwendigen Zusammenhang als Ursache mit der Glückseligkeit als Wirkung in der Sinnenwelt habe."

A noteworthy feature of this passage is the significance of the reference to the part played by the "Gesinnung", the subjective moral disposition; it is a feature which is continually emphasised in the rest of the "Dialectic".

Having stated his belief that, with the help of God, the creator both of the natural order, and of man as a moral being, it may be possible for morality (the "morality of the disposition") to have a necessary connection with happiness, Kant adds some remarks about the relation between morality and happiness in general. Epicurus, despite the emphasis that he places on pleasure, is not to be despised as a moral philosopher; for he commends unselfish conduct as a source of pleasure, and he advocates moderation and control of the natural inclinations ("Bändigung der Neigungen",115,219). But Kant criticises Epicurus for "presupposing a virtuous disposition" in a person (116,220), in order to be able to represent the person as capable of deriving pleasure from behaving virtuously. Such pleasure cannot produce a virtuous disposition; it can only arise from such a disposition.

The section dealing with "the primacy of pure

practical reason in its association with speculative reason" (119,223) is simply a reminder of a truth which Kant has long been concerned in the present work to impress upon us. It is particularly relevant in the "Dialectic", where happiness in the "Summum Bonum" is conditional upon morality inspired by pure practical reason. As Kant himself says, only if "practical reason were pathologically conditioned, merely attending to the interest of the inclinations in accordance with the sensuous principle of happiness", would practical reason forfeit its primacy to speculative reason. -"In der Tat, so fern praktische Vernunft als pathologisch bedingt, d.i. das Interesse der Neigungen unter dem sinnlichen Prinzip der Glückseligkeit bloß verwaltend, zum Grunde gelegt würde, so ließe sich diese Zumutung an die spekulative Vernunft gar nicht tun" (120,224).

Thus does Kant, engaged as he is in demonstrating the transcendence of practical reason, pause for a moment to remind us of the danger posed by natural inclinations to man's true moral destiny.

We come now to the section entitled "The immortality of the soul, as a postulate of pure practical reason" (122,225). Yet the idea of the immortality of the soul is merely incidental to Kant's principal theme, which is still the Highest Good. In fact it is also incidental to another idea which plays a key rôle in contributing to the Highest Good.

"The attainment of the Highest Good in the world is the necessary object of a will determinable by moral law. In this, however, the complete compatibility of the disposition with the moral law is the supreme condition of the Highest Good...But the complete compatibility of the will with the moral law is holiness, a perfection of which no rational being in the sensible world at any time in his existence is capable" (ibid).

So Kant refers both to the compatibility of the disposition (he uses the plural form of "Gesinnung", as he sometimes does), and to that of the will, with moral law. -"Die Bewirkung des höchsten Guts in der

Welt ist das notwendige Objekt eines durchs morali-
ische Gesetz bestimmbaren Willens. In diesem aber
ist die völlige Angemessenheit der Gesinnungen zum
moralischen Gesetze die oberste Bedingung des höchsten Guts...Die völlige Angemessenheit des Willens
aber zum moralischen Gesetze ist Heiligkeit, eine
Vollkommenheit deren kein vernünftiges Wesen der
Sinnenwelt in keinem Zeitpunkte seines Daseins fähig
ist." This is a passage of outstanding significance
in Kant's moral philosophy,because it is an explicit
statement of the importance to Kant of the compatibility of the subjective moral principle (b), whether this is represented by the "disposition" or the
"will", with principle (a), reason and moral law,
in their objectivity and universality. We should not
be surprised that Kant refers to the "compatibility"
("Angemessenheit") both of the "disposition" and of
the "will" with moral law. The virtue of the "good
will" was proclaimed at the beginning of the "Foundations", and the "Gesinnung" or "disposition" has
played an equally important part. Translators have
not always dealt very successfully with the latter
expression. It has a fixed and definite meaning in
Kant's text. It is a moral disposition, with only a
superficial analogy with "Neigung" ("inclination"),
because whereas an "inclination" belongs to the natural order, the "Gesinnung" belongs to the intelligible or noumenal world. If it is translated in various ways in different passages, as "character" or
"intention", or by whatever expression the translator's fancy happens to light on, the result is that
a key concept in Kant's philosophy is lost, as far
as the reader of the translation is concerned. As
regards the translation of "Angemessenheit" as "fit-
ness" instead of "compatibility", this probably be-
trays the translator's antipathy to the "compatibil-
ist" aspect of Kant's moral philosophy.

   But there is not the slightest doubt that Kant
believed that the higher principle of reason, and
the moral law produced by reason, must be supported
by man's subjective commitment, his sincere devotion

to moral law. Let us not forget the footnote (V.72, 180), in which Kant implied that if an action is carried out "for the sake of the law", and not mere- ly in conformity with it, then it is carried out "in the spirit" of the law, or with the required dispo- sition (the action is "dem Geiste, der Gesinnung nach moralisch gut"). It might be said that moral law is in a sense "given" to man (by his reason); what must be added is the subjective striving of the self, its giving of itself in support of moral law.

At this point Kant makes use of his continually repeated adage that if something, in a moral sense, "must" be done, it "can" be done, because as he im- plies it belongs to the providential arrangement of things. So here Kant says that the compatibility of the disposition with moral law must be possible, be- cause it is contained in the same commandment that requires man to strive to attain the Highest Good.

"Sie muß also eben sowohl möglich sein als ihr Objekt, weil sie in demselben Gebote dieses zu be- fördern enthalten ist" (122,225).

It is not the immortality of the soul in itself that concerns Kant in this passage, but the fact that man has infinite time in which to strive to at- tain the condition of "holiness", the condition in which the compatibility of the subjective moral dis- position with objective moral law,will be fulfilled. The attainment of the Highest Good is itself depen- dent on the striving of the moral "Gesinnung" to find a certain fulfilment in the moral law.

But Kant has already pointed out (supra p.69) that it is not possible for man to bring his subjec- tive self into complete agreement with objective moral law, and he reminds us of this truth in the present section, by explaining that "the complete compatibility of the will with moral law is holi- ness", a condition which God alone can attain. The disposition is "compatible" with moral law in the sense that it feels a certain affinity with it, a certain desire to act in accordance with it. But neither in this life, nor in the infinity of time that Kant envisages, can the action of the finite will ever agree perfectly with moral law. What it does in fact achieve is "the consciousness of its vindicated disposition" ("das Bewußtsein seiner erprüften Gesinnung", 123,226). What this means, to quote a phrase from Kant's footnote (123,227), is that it has acted "from sincere moral motives" ("aus echten, moralischen Bewegungsgründen"). This is as good a definition of the moral "Gesinnung" as one could hope for.

As for the will's aim of participating in the fullness of time in the Highest Good, Kant points out that the slow progress of the finite soul from the lower to the higher stages of perfection,is seen differently by God. For he, in a single intuition, sees in that slow progress, as its total effect, the soul's compatibility with moral law. -"Der Unendliche, dem die Zeitbedingung Nichts ist, sieht in dieser für uns endlosen Reihe das Ganze der Angemessenheit mit dem moralischen Gesetze" (123,226). It is undoubtedly by virtue of his understanding of the complete sincerity of the disposition, that God is able to make such a favourable judgment.

We come now to the section entitled "The Existence of God as a postulate of pure practical reason" (124,227). As we have already seen, if we are to believe in the Highest Good, we must also believe in the existence of God as the author of the natural world, who can bring about the "exact agreement of happiness with morality" ("die genaue Übereinstimmung der Glückseligkeit mit der Sittlichkeit",125, 228). As in the previous section, Kant stresses the part played by the subjective disposition (the "Gesinnung") in giving a reliable indication of the moral condition of the person concerned.

"The supreme cause (by which Kant refers to God) must contain the ground of the agreement of nature, not merely with a law of the will of rational beings, but with the idea of this law, so far as they make it the supreme ground of the determination of their will, that is, not merely with the formal aspect of morality, but with their morality as their motive, that is, with their moral disposition ("Gesinnung"). Thus the Highest Good in the world is possible only on the supposition of a supreme cause of nature, having a causality corresponding to the moral disposition ("Gesinnung")" (ibid).

"Diese oberste Ursache aber soll den Grund der Übereinstimmung der Natur nicht bloß mit einem Gesetze des Willens der vernünftigen Wesen, sondern mit der Vorstellung dieses Gesetzes, so fern diese es sich zum obersten Bestimmungsgrunde des Willens setzen, also nicht bloß mit den Sitten der Form nach, sondern auch ihrer Sittlichkeit als dem Bewegungsgrunde derselben, d.i. mit ihrer moralischen Gesinnung, enthalten. Also ist das höchste Gut in der Welt nur möglich, so fern eine oberste Ursache der Natur angenommen wird, die eine der moralischen Gesinnung gemäße Kausalität hat."

It is impossible to overestimate the importance of such a passage. Of course the people referred to are "rational beings", and reason gives them the moral law, principle (a); but what Kant picks out as of supreme importance is their inner "motive", their profound dedication to morality, their indwelling moral "disposition", principle (b). Needless to say, this is exactly the kind of passage in which the key idea of the "disposition", is watered down in translation by the use of some other expression.

In discussing the Christian teaching concerning the Highest Good (the kingdom of God), Kant finds that it has much in common with his own moral philosophy. "The moral law is holy, i.e. strict, and requires holiness in morality, although such moral perfection as man can achieve, is never more than virtue, i.e. a law-abiding disposition from respect for the law, therefore consciousness of a continual tendency to transgression, at least impurity, that is, an admixture of many false motives for obeying the law, consequently a self-judgment associated with humility, and so with respect to the holiness required by Christian law, leaving to God's creature only (the prospect of) progress ad infinitum, but for that reason justifying the hope of his continued existence ad infinitum. The value of a disposition completely compatible with the moral law is infinite; because all the possible happiness in the judgment of a wise and omnipotent bestower of happiness is limited only by the lack of compatibility between rational beings and their duty" (128,231).

In this section, where Kant is concerned with the happiness which the virtuous person looks forward to experiencing in the condition known as the Highest Good, it is necessary that he should issue a warning that, although happiness may be the reward for observing the moral law, the desire for happiness should not be the agent's motive in observing the law. By virtue of our moral disposition, we act according to the law for its own sake. In this way Kant safeguards the principle of autonomy with respect to the moral disposition.

He safeguards the principle of autonomy in another way too. Although the moral law, through the idea of the Highest Good, leads to the recognition of all duties as divine commandments, this does not mean that they are "sanctions,i.e. arbitrary or contingent ordinances of an alien will" (129,232). On the contrary, they are "essentially laws of each free will for itself; which must nevertheless be regarded as commandments of the supreme being" (ibid), because it is only by means of a morally perfect and omnipotent God, that we can hope to attain the Highest Good. Therefore Kant maintains that Christian belief, as well as his own moral philosophy, is not what he calls "theological, consequently heteronomy, but the autonomy of pure practical reason for itself". -"Diesem ungeachtet ist das christliche Prinzip der Moral selbst doch nicht theologisch (mithin Heteronomie), sondern Autonomie der reinen praktischen Vernunft für sich selbst..." (129,232).

In view of this emphasis on the principle of autonomy, it is appropriate that Kant should conclude the section by affirming his belief that man

is an end in himself. "It follows of itself that our
humanity must be holy to us, because man is the subject of the moral law, which in itself is holy...For
this moral law is founded on the autonomy of his
will, as a free will, which at the same time according to its universal laws must necessarily be able
to agree with that to which it is under an obligation to submit itself."

"Daß also die Menschheit in unserer Person uns
selbst heilig sein müsse, folgt nunmehr von selbst,
weil er das Subjekt des moralischen Gesetzes, mithin
dessen ist, was an sich heilig ist...Denn dieses
moralische Gesetz gründet sich auf der Autonomie
seines Willens, der nach seinen allgemeinen Gesetzen
notwendig zu demjenigen zugleich muß einstimmen können, welchem er sich unterwerfen soll" (131f,234).

Thus Kant's often repeated statement that if a
man "ought" to do something, he must also have the
"ability" to do it, is now interpreted as meaning
that if Providence has placed him under an obligation to do something, it must also have given him
the ability to do it by agreement with his own imma-
ment moral disposition.

The next section that we must deal with is entitled "Of Belief from a need of pure reason" (142,
243). Kant explains his argument as follows. "A need
of pure practical reason is based on a duty of making something (the Highest Good) the object of my
will, in order to promote it with all my strength.
In doing so, I must presuppose its possibility and
also its conditions, namely God, freedom and immortality; because I cannot prove these by my speculative reason, although I cannot refute them either"
(142,244). In other words, Kant considers whether he
is justified in his belief in the Highest Good, God,
freedom and immortality, even though he receives no
support from speculative reason for his belief in
these things. It is the moral law that obliges him
to hold these beliefs.

"But the subjective effect of this law, namely the
disposition which is compatible with it, and which

is made necessary by it, of promoting the practically possible Highest Good, at least presupposes that
the latter is possible." -"Aber der subjektive Ef-
fekt dieses Gesetzes, nämlich die ihm angemessene
und durch dasselbe auch notwendige Gesinnung, das
praktisch mögliche höchste Gut zu befördern, setzt
doch wenigstens voraus, daß das letztere möglich
sei" (143,244). Although the condition of "holiness"
can never be actually achieved, in a sense the act
of striving for the Highest Good is in itself worth
while, if it demonstrates that the disposition is at
least worthy of the Highest Good.

    Although speculative reason lends the man of
faith no support, he is impelled both by his respect
for objective moral law and by his subjective moral
disposition, to declare: "I will that there shall be
a God, that my existence in this world shall also be
an existence in a pure world of the understanding,
outside the world of natural connections, and finally that my duration shall be endless. I stand by
this, and will not let this faith be taken from me;
for this is the one thing, in which my interest inevitably determines my judgment, because I may not
give up one iota of it" (143,245). The person concerned, in stating that he "may" not give up any of
his faith ("weil ich von demselben nichts nachlassen
darf"), means that he is not permitted by his own
respect for moral law, to give up his faith in the
Highest Good. Since speculative reason does not make
any firm pronouncement concerning this article of
faith, Kant suggests that we should leave it to our
moral "interest" to decide in favour of it (V.145,
246). In a final remark he states that such faith in
the Highest Good, the faith of pure practical reason, as he calls it, may well arise from the "moral
disposition" ("selbst aus der moralischen Gesinnung
entsprungen",146,247). It is a faith that may perhaps waver "even in well-disposed persons" ("selbst
bei Wohlgesinnten"), but will scarcely ever give way
to unbelief.

    None of these sections that we have been exam-
ining could be more important than the last, which

is entitled "Of the wise application of man's cogni-
tive faculties to his practical vocation" (146,247).
Kant invites us to imagine what it would have been
like if our desire to experience the Highest Good
more directly, had actually been satisfied, as Kant
seems to imply, while we were still on earth. First
our natural inclinations would have demanded satisfaction, in the name of "happiness"; and the moral
law would have spoken later, in order to restrain
the inclinations. "But instead of the war which the
moral disposition now has to wage with the inclinations, a war in which after several reverses, the
moral strength of the soul gradually prevails, God
and eternity would continually confront us, in all
their fearful majesty" (147,248).

"Aber statt des Streits, den jetzt die moralische Gesinnung mit den Neigungen zu führen hat, in
welchem nach einigen Niederlagen doch allmählich
moralische Stärke der Seele zu erwerben ist, würden
Gott und Ewigkeit mit ihrer furchtbaren Majestät uns
unablässig vor Augen liegen..."

The passage serves to remind us of the need to
distinguish clearly between the natural inclination
(the "Neigung") on the one hand, and on the other
hand the moral "disposition" (the "Gesinnung"),which
belongs to the intelligible world,the world of reason and moral law. That is an elementary, but also an
essential point. The main point is of course the
striving of the indwelling moral disposition in its
attempt to restrain the inclinations. Kant contrasts
this inner moral struggle of the disposition, with
the mere external sanctions that would be imposed,
if as he has said, we were to be overawed by the
actual presence of God. Although transgression of
the law would be avoided, the "spur of action" would
not arise from the inner self.

"Die Übertretung des Gesetzes würde freilich
vermieden, das Gebotene getan werden; weil aber die
Gesinnung, aus welcher Handlungen geschehen sollen,
durch kein Gebot mit eingeflößt werden kann, der
Stachel der Tätigkeit hier aber sogleich bei Hand

und äußerlich ist, die Vernunft also sich nicht allererst empor arbeiten darf, um Kraft zum Widerstande
gegen Neigungen durch lebendige Vorstellung der Würde des Gesetzes zu sammeln, so würden die mehrsten
gesetzmäßigen Handlungen aus Furcht, nur wenige aus
Hoffnung und gar keine aus Pflicht geschehen, ein
moralischer Wert der Handlungen aber, worauf doch
allein der Wert der Person und selbst der der Welt
in den Augen der höchsten Weisheit ankommt, würde
gar nicht existieren" (147,248).

Kant strongly emphasises the importance of the
inner moral motivation. We are told that "actions
should take place from the (motive of the inner)
disposition" ("die Gesinnung, aus welcher Handlungen
geschehen sollen"). The moral disposition is innate;
it cannot be imparted by any commandment ("weil aber
die Gesinnung...durch kein Gebot mit eingeflößt werden kann"). Indeed Kant maintains that the moral
value of the actions, and of the agent performing
them, is derived essentially from the inner motive
of the indwelling moral disposition.

It is a remarkable fact that in a work dedicated
mainly to reason and moral law, principle (a), Kant
should still find it appropriate to pay this impressive tribute to the inner moral disposition, principle (b). We are strongly reminded of the "good will"
at the beginning of the "Foundations",and even more,
in the same work, of the key passage (432f,90) where
the law is described, according to the principle of
autonomy, as arising from our own will. What is emphasised in these two passages, whether Kant is referring to the "will" or the "disposition" (both exemplifying principle "b"), is the spontaneity of the
inner impulse, which ensures that the law "arises
from our own will", or that the "spur of activity"
is provided by the indwelling moral disposition.

If, says Kant, in the actual presence of God,
we were reduced to acting from such "external" motives as "fear" and "hope", our actions would be
merely mechanical; in fact we would resemble puppets
or marionettes, capable of gesticulating,but without
life (147,248).

However, since God does not in fact reveal himself to us, we are obliged to rely on our own moral resources. "Only in this way can there be a true moral disposition, dedicated directly as it is to the law, and a rational being can become worthy of a share in the Highest Good, a share that corresponds to the moral worth of the person, and not only to his actions." -"So kann wahrhafte sittliche, dem Gesetze unmittelbar geweihte Gesinnung stattfinden, und das vernünftige Geschöpf des Anteils am höchsten Gute würdig werden, das dem moralischen Werte seiner Person und nicht bloß seinen Handlungen angemessen ist" (147f,248).

Kant could hardly have made his meaning clearer. First, the moral worth of a person cannot be measured simply by his outward actions. But second, his true inner moral worth is to be measured, not merely by his possession of the moral law given to him by his reason, but also by his possession of a moral disposition, dedicated to the moral law.

The part played by the moral disposition, both in the "Foundations" and in the "Critique", has generally speaking been underestimated by critics.

# CHAPTER THREE

## RELIGION WITHIN THE LIMITS OF REASON, 1793

The pleonastic German title, "Religion inner-
halb der Grenzen der bloßen Vernunft", need not be
taken as an excuse for equally pleonastic English
titles, such as "Religion within the Limits of Reason itself", or "Reason alone". In one sense it is
not even true that Kant limits his discussion of
religion to the rational side of it; for in this
work, as in the rest of his moral philosophy, he is
concerned just as much with the moral disposition
(the "Gesinnung") as with reason. But what his title
implies is that he is concerned mainly with religion
as embodying the morality of reason,as distinct from
"revealed" religion. The title indicates that for
Kant religion is above all "natural" religion, that
is, a religion developed from reason rather than by
"revelation".

As Kant himself says, in both types of religion
we recognise our duties as divine commands; the difference is that in natural religion we are possessed
of a certain faculty (reason) which enables us to
see for ourselves that a certain principle must be
accepted as unconditional; whereas in revealed religion it must first be revealed to us as a divine
command, before we can accept it as our duty. -"Religion ist (subjektiv betrachtet) das Erkenntnis
aller unserer Pflichten als göttlicher Gebote. Diejenige, in welcher ich vorher wissen muß, daß etwas
ein göttliches Gebot sei, um es als meine Pflicht
anzuerkennen, ist die geoffenbarte...Religion: dagegen diejenige, in der ich zuvor wissen muß, daß
etwas Pflicht sei, ehe ich es für ein göttliches Gebot anerkennen kann, ist die natürliche Religion"
(VI.153f).

The affinity between human reason and divine
law is still further emphasised when Kant, in referring to moral principles, declares that everyone, by
employing his own innate reason ("aus sich selbst"),
can know the will of God; for the very concept of
God arises only from our consciousness of his laws.

"In Ansehung der letztern kann ein jeder aus sich selbst durch seine eigene Vernunft den Willen Gottes...erkennen; denn eigentlich entspringt der Begriff von der Gottheit nur aus dem Bewußtsein dieser Gesetze" (VI.104).

But God is immanent in us, not merely through our moral principles, corresponding to God's commands; he is also present in us in our moral disposition, which predisposes us to accept and act on those principles or commands. The disposition (or the "Gesinnung") plays a not less important part in the "Religion" than in the "Dialectic". We have seen that from Kant's point of view the principle of "pure nature", as a prospective subjective moral principle, is discredited by association with empiricism. The inner moral disposition does not suffer from any such disqualification. While Kant has been firmly maintaining his opposition, not only to the self-indulgent type of natural inclination, but also to such natural inclinations as fall under the heading of "pure nature", he has at the same time been quietly cultivating the idea of the moral disposition, assigning to it a key part in the "Dialectic", where it serves as the principle by which God himself judges whether a person is morally worthy of happiness in accordance with the concept of the "Summum Bonum".

In the "Religion" itself there are many passages where the main emphasis is on the "inwardness" of the moral disposition. In fact, if we take into account, not only the moral laws produced by reason, but also the part played by the moral disposition, we might well conclude that a better title for this work would have been "Religion within the Limits of Morality"; because morality includes not only reason, principle (a), but also the moral disposition, principle (b), with both of which Kant is concerned.

It is in Chapter Four of the "Religion" that Kant deals specifically with the distinction between a "revealed" and a "natural" religion, i.e. between a religion based on the teaching of a divinely inspired religious leader, and on the other hand a

religion that is "natural" in the sense that it is
based on the reason that is "natural" to man. Kant
implies that from his point of view the value of revealed religion consists in the opportunity that it
offers for a religion of pure morality based on universal reason to develop from it. In fact he maintains that a revealed religion should contain a
principle which will enable it to move ever closer
to the "pure faith of reason" ("sich dem reinen Ver-
nunftglauben...beständig zu nähern",VI.153).

As we have already mentioned, Kant also speaks
of the moral disposition as playing an important
part. For instance he quotes Matthew V.20-48, where
Jesus declares that it is not merely by external
acts of worship that a person can please God, but
even more (in Kant's words) by the "pure moral disposition of the heart" ("die reine moralische Herzensgesinnung",VI.159).

The importance of the inner moral disposition
is also illustrated by Matthew V.28, where it is
stated that to sin "in one's heart" is to sin before
God, even without the deed. It is also illustrated
by Matthew V.24, where the act of placing a gift before the altar is described as of less importance
than the duty of effecting a reconciliation with
one's brother. In a footnote (VI.160) Kant adds that
the narrow gate and the strait way which lead to
life represent the morally good way of life; and
that the wide gate and the broad way which many pass
through, represent the kind of church which in his
opinion attaches too much importance to external
observances. But he also explains that, if people
are morally confused, this is only because they fail
to understand that it is mainly by leading a good
life that they can serve God.

In the section entitled "The Christian religion
as a learned religion" (VI.163) Kant makes a clear
distinction between Christianity as a revealed or
"learned" religion, and Christianity as a "natural"
religion, the religion of moral law based on reason.
Despite the love and esteem enjoyed by a small band

of scholars devoted to the study of Christianity as
a "revealed" religion, that aspect of it is after
all only a means to an end, the development of a religion of morality based on reason. That is the true
function of the church; but if faith in revelation
takes precedence over true religion, it becomes a
spurious cult. What was only the means, becomes the
end (VI.165).

Kant represents what he regards as the spurious
cultic aspect of religion as offensive to the true
rational-moral spirit that should inform a religion.
"True religion", he says, "contains nothing but laws
...which we recognise as revealed to us by pure
reason, not empirically". -"Die wahre, alleinige Religion enthält nichts als Gesetze...die wir also als
durch reine Vernunft (nicht empirisch) offenbart anerkennen" (VI.167).

But Kant is even more insistent on the sharp
contrast between certain perverse practices, as exemplified in certain religions, on the one hand, and
on the other the inestimable value of a sincere moral "disposition". Such a disposition, "which enables
us to lead a morally good life" (VI.172), is far
more effective in pleasing God than all the rigours
and hardship suffered, for instance, by those who
went on pilgrimages or performed perverse acts of
atonement (VI.168). A monk or hermit, lost to the
world, offered up to God a life of self-sacrifice;
the only thing that he did not offer up was his moral disposition ("Er bringt alles, nur nicht seine
moralische Gesinnung Gott dar",VI.172). In another
passage Kant declares that there can be nothing in
common between worshipping God with your moral disposition (including the moral behaviour that follows
from such a disposition), and on the other hand
attempting to gain his approval by the kind of chil-
dish observances that are practised in some of the
world's religions ("Gott entweder nur durch moralische Gesinnung, so fern sie sich in Handlungen als
ihrer Erscheinung als lebendig darstellt, oder durch
frommes Spielwerk und Nichtstuerei wohlgefällig zu
zu werden" (VI.173).

Just as Kant, in his general moral philosophy, distinguishes between the inestimable value of the morally good inner disposition on the one hand, and on the other mere outward conformity to moral law, so in his "Religion" he exalts the genuine moral disposition, whether it takes the form of moral purity or of sincere repentance, above all external religious observances and acts of expiation. No such acts, no paeans in praise of God, are any substitute for a genuine feeling of repentance; only by a "complete change of heart" can a person who is burdened with guilt obtain absolution from God. -"Denn man sieht...daß nur unter der Voraussetzung der gänzlichen Herzensänderung sich für den mit Schuld belasteten Menschen vor der himmlischen Gerechtigkeit Lossprechung denken lasse" (VI.76).

It is mainly in Chapter 3, entitled "The victory of the good principle over the evil one, and the establishment of a kingdom of God on earth" (VI.93), that Kant describes the process by which a "pure religion of reason" ("reine Vernunftreligion",VI.121) is to develop. As in other parts of the "Religion", it is not only the key word "Vernunft" (reason) that echoes through these pages, but also that other key word "Gesinnung" (the moral disposition). The religion that is to be developed is to be above all a moral religion, which will have to rise above the existing institutions (a church based on revealed religion and a civil society). The moral character of the new religion is to be seen from the perspective of both those institutions.

Kant begins with a reference to the contrast drawn by Rousseau between the "moral predisposition" ("moralische Anlage") or natural morality, which man enjoyed so long as he was left to himself, and the process by which he was corrupted by envy and "hostile inclinations" as soon as he came into contact with other people living in a community. "It is easy for man to persuade himself that this danger does not arise from his own crude nature ("von seiner eigenen rohen Natur",VI.93), but from the people with whom he comes in contact." Kant is probably right to question Rousseau's belief that it is only by coming into contact with "society" that people are corrupted. Envy, greed and hostility are latent in every individual; it is simply that such latent characteristics are brought to the surface in his relations with other people. But Kant's main point is that envy, greed and hostility must be opposed in the name of morality. Therefore reason, in addition to the moral laws which it prescribes for each individual, must also so to speak raise a "banner of virtue", to rally and unite all those who love what is good, and so to form an ethical community or a church. "Es ist von der moralischgesetzgebenden Vernunft außer den Gesetzen, die sie jedem Einzelnen vorschreibt, noch überdem eine Fahne der Tugend als Vereinigungspunkt für alle, die das Gute lieben, ausgesteckt" (VI.93f). Only by the formation of such an ethical community can the tragic moral effect of the Hobbesian "status belli omnium in omnes" be avoided (VI.97fn).

Such an "ethical" community, as distinct from a civil community, must be based on "laws of virtue" ("Tugendgesetzen",VI.94), and so will form a "kingdom of virtue" ("ein Reich der Tugend",VI.95).

In comparing a civil society with an ethical community, Kant takes as an example of the former Rousseau's account of the society in which the liberty of every individual is so limited as to make it compatible with the liberty of every other individual, in agreement with the principle of the "general will" (VI.98). The laws which govern the ethical community do not involve coercion such as is imposed by the general will in a civil society; whereas in the latter the authorities are concerned only with the external legality of the citizens' actions, the laws which govern the ethical community are the inner laws of morality. -"Denn in einem solchen gemeinen Wesen sind alle Gesetze ganz eigentlich darauf gestellt, die Moralität der Handlungen (welche etwas Innerliches ist...) zu befördern..." (VI.98).

Evidence that Kant is thinking of the "kingdom of virtue" in terms, not only of "reason", but also of the inner subjective "disposition" ("Gesinnung") soon accumulates. He emphasises that the forces of evil are not to be thought of as external to ourselves, but as within us. It is only in a figurative sense that we are justified in speaking of them as an external hostile army, opposed to our "virtuous dispositions". -"Einem solchen Volke Gottes kann man die Idee einer Rotte des bösen Prinzips entgegensetzen...wiewohl auch hier das die Tugendgesinnungen anfechtende Prinzip gleichfalls in uns selbst liegt und nur bildlich als äußere Macht vorgestellt wird" (VI.100). When Kant quotes from the Lord's prayer the reference to the coming of God's kingdom, and to the fulfilment of his will on earth as in heaven, he describes this as "the wish of all well-disposed people" ("der Wunsch aller Wohlgesinnten",VI.101).

Both reason and the subjective "disposition" are shown by Kant to play a part in the development of a moral religion from a religion which began as an "historical" or revealed religion. In general, religions have to take account of the innate tendency in human beings to remain close to whatever is tangible, and to keep their thoughts from moving too far away from the sensible world surrounding them ("wegen des natürlichen Bedürfnisses aller Menschen, zu den höchsten Vernunftbegriffen und Gründen immer etwas Sinnlich-Haltbares...zu verlangen",VI.109). Yet it is precisely the ability to rise above the level of the empirical world that is required by a religion of pure reason, based as it must be on the universality and the necessity of the moral laws produced by reason. Here then reason has a vital part to play, in attempting to overcome the limitations of human nature, and in raising people's minds above the merely empirical level. On the other hand it is to the indwelling moral disposition that Kant appeals, when he deprecates the tendency to base religion on mere external observances, or on the sort of "cult" which he regards as morally worthless.

"Denn dieser muß ein freier, auf lautere Herz-
ensgesinnungen gegründeter Glaube (fides ingenua)
sein. Der erstere wähnt durch Handlungen (des cul-
tus), welche (obzwar mühsam) doch für sich keinen
moralischen Wert haben...Gott wohlgefällig zu werden, anstatt daß der letztere dazu eine moralisch
gute Gesinnung als notwendig voraussetzt" (VI.115f).

If a revealed, or as Kant refers to it, an empirical faith, which has been handed down to us, is
to serve as the basis for a truly moral faith, then
it needs to be "interpreted" (VI.110). A few pages
further on Kant gives us an example of the kind of
interpretation that he would put upon a particular
doctrine of revealed religion. He refers to the doctrine that it is only by believing that Jesus has
atoned for the sins of all mankind (or as Kant puts
it, their negligence in doing their moral duty),
that mankind can be saved (VI.120).

Kant interprets this doctrine, in the light of
reason, in the following passage. -"Man muß mit all-
en Kräften der heiligen Gesinnung eines Gott wohlge-
fälligen Lebenswandels nachstreben, um glauben zu
können, daß die (uns schon durch die Vernunft ver-
sicherte) Liebe desselben zur Menschheit, sofern sie
seinem Willen nach allem ihrem Vermögen nachstrebt,
in Rücksicht auf die redliche Gesinnung den Mangel
der Tat, auf welche Art es auch sei,ergänzen werde."

Kant implies that although we can never make
our disposition agree completely with the moral law,
nor by doing so equal God's "holy" disposition,
nevertheless if the soul strives through infinite
time to achieve just such a perfect agreement, by
leading a life that is pleasing to God, we may still
believe what our reason assures us of - that He, in
His love of mankind, so long as we strive to do His
will with all our power, "will in consideration of
our sincere disposition, make good any deficiency,
of whatever kind it may be, in our actual deeds".

As regards the reference to God's "holy disposition", this confirms the statement in the "Critique" that man can only strive to emulate the holiness of God (V.83,190 and 84,191).

In the passage quoted Kant shifts the emphasis somewhat from the part played by Jesus in atoning for the sins of mankind, to the attempt made by man himself to act in agreement with moral law. But Kant seeks to combine the two things: God's love of man, and man's efforts to save himself by leading a life that is pleasing to God. God judges man by his inner motive, by the sincerity of his disposition. God's "grace" is not an unmerited gift, but a recognition of the sincerity of man's disposition, and a corresponding willingness to make good the shortfall of his actual deeds. Kant's word for this is "ergänzen", i.e. to "complement", by taking the will for the deed.

So Kant confirms his remarks in the "Critique" concerning the striving of man's immortal soul for ever greater moral perfection. But now he is also pleading for a greater recognition of the truth that salvation for man depends, not only on God's grace, but also on the striving of man's disposition to lead a life that is pleasing to God.

The part played by the "disposition" in this passage is obvious, but at the same time it is reason which reinterprets the message of revealed religion by freeing it of its empirical origins. "Thus religion must be gradually freed from all empirical factors, from all statutes which are based on history, and which provisionally unite people in promoting what is good; and so the pure religion of reason ultimately prevails over all" (VI.121). In this context Kant refers to the enveloping vestiges of the revealed religion which, having protected the embryo of the true religion until it matures, must then be discarded. -"Die Hüllen, unter welchen der Embryo sich zuerst zum Menschen bildete, müssen abgelegt werden, wenn er nun an das Tageslicht treten soll" (ibid). It is a time of change, in a sense of moral "revolution", but "without anarchy". Thus Kant contrasts the gradual and peaceful change which reason is bringing about in the maturing of the church, with the violence and the excesses of the French

Revolution, occurring at that time. In order to explain the peaceful character of the process of re-
interpreting the faith of the church, Kant invokes
his own principle of "autonomy", according to which
"everyone obeys the non-statutory law which he prescribes for himself, but which at the same time he
must regard as the will of God who rules the world,
a will revealed to him by reason". All are now united in a universal kingdom, which is "invisible" or
spiritual, a kingdom which was previously inade-
quately represented, and yet prepared for, by the
visible church.   -"Der erniedrigende Unterschied
zwischen Laien und Klerikern hört auf, und Gleich-
heit entspringt aus der wahren Freiheit, jedoch ohne
Anarchie, weil ein jeder zwar dem (nicht statutar-
ischen) Gesetz gehorcht, das er sich selbst vorschreibt, das er aber auch zugleich als den ihm
durch die Vernunft geoffenbarten Willen des Welt-
herrschers ansehen muß, der alle unter einer gemeinschaftlichen Regierung unsichtbarer Weise in einem
Staate verbindet, welcher durch die sichtbare Kirche
vorher dürftig vorgestellt und vorbereitet war".
    In this passage (VI.122) Kant discovers a dif-
ferent kind of "revealed" religion: not the original
one, based on the past historical circumstances, but
the discovery of the moral implications "revealed by
reason" ("durch die Vernunft geoffenbart") in the
existing religion. He again speaks in terms of this
different type of revelation, when he looks ahead to
a "new order of things" which will arise from the
"religion of pure reason" as "a divine, but not empirical revelation, which will be continually granted to all men".
    "In diesem Prinzip der reinen Vernunftreligion,
als einer an alle Menschen beständig geschehenden
göttlichen (obzwar nicht empirischen) Offenbarung,
muß der Grund zu jenem Überschritt zu jener neuen
Ordnung der Dinge liegen" (VI.122).
    An important feature of Kant's "Religion" is his
use of the word "Willkür" in the sense of the "elective will". We have seen that in the "Critique of

Practical Reason" the word "Willkür" was applied to
the will that was particularly subject to natural
inclinations (supra p.49), including perhaps a crude
inclination ("crude nature"), presumably because
action which is "willkürlich" is "arbitrary" or by
extension "lawless". But in the "Religion" the word
"Willkür" refers to the will's responsibility for
making a deliberate "choice" or decision (cf. "Kur-
fürst", referring to an "elector" in the German
empire). The freedom or "spontaneity" of the will
(based on its responsibility for making a moral
choice) is described as follows. "The freedom of the
will has the peculiar characteristic that it cannot
be determined by any motive to take action, unless
the person concerned has adopted it as his maxim
(has made it his universal rule, according to which
he will act); only in this way can a motive, whatever it may be, prove compatible with the absolute
spontaneity of the will (i.e. with freedom)"(VI.23).

"Die Freiheit der Willkür ist von der ganz eig-
entümlichen Beschaffenheit, daß sie durch keine
Triebfeder zu einer Handlung bestimmt werden kann,
als nur sofern der Mensch sie in seine Maxime aufgenommen hat (es sich zur allgemeinen Regel gemacht
hat, nach der er sich verhalten will): so allein
kann eine Triebfeder, welche sie auch sei, mit der
absoluten Spontaneität der Willkür (der Freiheit)
zusammen bestehen."

In the "Religion" the will is above all a principle which is able to choose between one motive and
another, consciously and deliberately taking one
motive up into its maxim, and rejecting another.
Thus the will is characterised above all by the fact
that it is "accountable" or responsible for its decisions and the resulting actions, which are "attri-
butable" to it, whether they are good or bad. Although the will has the duty of acting in conformity
with moral law, this does not mean that the agent
does not sometimes give way to natural inclination,
and so begins to act "of necessity", in a way that
conflicts with the law. When Kant, in the "Foundations",describes the will as subject both to natural

inclination and to moral law, he implies that when it acts from natural inclination, it has yielded to it and is responsible for yielding to it. There is no "necessity" about the action by which the will adopts an inclination as its maxim, because the will has the faculty of reason which enables it to reject natural inclination. Necessity enters into it only after the will has consciously yielded to inclination. From then onward, unless it consciously decides to change its maxim, it acts according to instinct or the process of natural necessity.

The theory that the will is free either to adopt a motive as its maxim, or not, has been described as the "incorporation thesis". But this expression, not usually employed by Kant himself, tends to give the false impression that it represents something new, introduced for the first time in the "Religion". To "incorporate" a motive is simply to adopt it as a maxim, and in all Kant's major works he attributes to the will the ability to decide whether in this way to adopt a motive or not. He has never suggested that the will has no choice but to act from natural inclination. All that he does in this regard in the "Religion" is to give still greater emphasis to the freedom and accountability of the will that he has always insisted on. So we must not think of the "incorporation thesis" as a kind of transformation that has overtaken the will.

There is however a much greater transformation that the will has in fact undergone. At the beginning of the "Foundations" the "good" will was an exemplification of principle (b), an indwelling moral principle which played much the same rôle as that of the disposition itself, its function being to support reason and moral law, principle (a). Since then however the will has assumed other functions, in the light of which it has undergone a transformation which has occurred in two stages.

In the "Foundations", by virtue of the principle of autonomy (which was implied in all the formulations of the categorical imperative, but which was

specifically stated in the formula of universal law
and in that of autonomy itself), the will acquired
the "unconditional" character that is typical of
reason itself (supra p.37f.). In this way,as we have
already pointed out (supra p.31), Kant in the "Foundations" exalts the will to a level almost equal to
that of reason itself.

The second stage in the transformation of the
will occurred in the "Critique". Whereas in the
"Foundations" the will derived its autonomous character precisely from its own indwelling moral impulse, which was the very factor which rendered its
adoption of the moral law "unconditional", in the
"Critique" on the other hand it was with the autonomy of reason, the principle presiding over the noumenal world, and triumphantly defying the world of
nature, that Kant was mainly concerned. Nevertheless
the will was closely associated with the autonomy of
reason; so that Kant was able to maintain that "in
the concept of a pure will the concept of causality
with freedom is already contained" (supra p.55).

We should therefore not be surprised to find
that in the "Religion" the will should appear as a
fully accredited representative of principle (a),
the principle of reason and moral law.

We have seen that the "disposition" (the "Gesinnung"), the representative in the "Religion", as
in the two earlier works, of principle (b), exists
so to speak as an innate moral character in the person concerned. Yet it seems that Kant's purpose in
this work is to bring the moral disposition into relation with the "Willkür", which as we have already
explained, represents principle (a). Indeed Kant believes that, in some inscrutable way, every moral
disposition, despite its appearance of being "natural" or "innate", must have been freely acquired.

"When it is said that a man has the one or the
other disposition as an innate quality, this does
not mean that it has not been acquired by the person
possessing it, nor that he is not the author of it;
but only that it has not been acquired in time (that

he has always, from his youth upward, been one or the other). The disposition, i.e. the first subjective principle of the adoption of maxims, can be but one, and applies generally to the whole use of freedom. But it must itself have been adopted by free will; for otherwise it could not be attributed.Nothing more of the subjective principle or cause of its adoption can be known (although we cannot help inquiring about it,since otherwise another maxim would have to be adduced, by which the disposition had been adopted, which in turn would have to have its principle or cause). Since therefore we cannot deduce this disposition, or rather its ultimate principle, from any first act of the will in time, we call it a characteristic of the will belonging to it by nature (although in fact it is founded on freedom)." -"Die eine oder die andere Gesinnung als angeborne Beschaffenheit von Natur haben,bedeutet hier auch nicht, daß sie von dem Menschen, der sie hegt, gar nicht erworben, d.i. er nicht Urheber sei (daß er eines oder das andere von Jugend auf sei immerdar). Die Gesinnung, d.i. der erste subjektive Grund der Annehmung der Maximen, kann nur eine einzige sein, und geht allgemein auf den ganzen Gebrauch der Freiheit. Sie selbst aber muß auch durch freie Willkür angenommen worden sein, denn sonst könnte sie nicht zugerechnet werden. Von dieser Annehmung kann nicht wieder der subjektive Grund oder die Ursache erkannt werden (obwohl darnach zu fragen unvermeidlich ist: weil sonst wiederum eine Maxime angeführt werden müßte, in welche diese Gesinnung aufgenommen worden, die eben so wiederum ihren Grund haben muß). Weil wir also diese Gesinnnung, oder vielmehr ihren obersten Grund nicht von irgendeinem ersten Zeit-Actus der Willkür ableiten können, so nennen wir sie eine Beschaffenheit der Willkür, die ihr (ob sie gleich in der Tat in der Freiheit gegründet ist) von Natur zukommt" (VI.25).

In this passage Kant makes it clear that the moral disposition is not to be regarded simply as an innate propensity tending to morality, but that

the choice or the decision that is made is "attribu-
table" to the person whose attribute it is. In the
context of this passage the two principles, the disposition and the rational-moral principle may be regarded as representing two different concepts of the
self. In the "Foundations", particularly in the key
passage (IV.432,90), the idea of moral law arising
from a moral principle immanent in our own will, as
opposed to moral law imposed by transcendent reason,
gives us the idea of a self based on our own disposition, and acting on moral law spontaneously, as
though by our very nature. If on the other hand we
dissociate ourselves from the disposition as from a
set attitude given to us by nature, and acting im-
personally within us, then we can the more readily
recognise the conscious rational-moral principle as
the true self. In the first case we identify our
self with the moral disposition within us,from which
arises our moral impulse; in the second case we
identify our self with the elective will, through
whose moral decisions we control our own moral destiny. The implication of the passage quoted (VI.25)
is that each of these selves is essential to the
other. Both principles serve the same purpose, that
of ensuring that the will shall act in accordance
with and for the sake of moral law. Principle (a),
the "Willkür", seeks to bring this about by consciously choosing a motive which agrees with moral
law; principle (b) relies upon the inner moral disposition to prevail upon the will to commit itself
to moral law. So the two principles complement each
other.

There is a certain aspect of the moral disposition which appears more clearly in the "Religion"
than in Kant's earlier works. It is perhaps the emotional quality characteristic of religious awareness
that causes Kant to refer to the moral disposition
in terms of the "heart". We have already quoted two
references to the "disposition of the heart", the
"Herzensgesinnung", VI.159 and VI.115 (supra pp.101
and 106), and a reference to a "change of heart", a
"Herzensänderung", VI.76 (supra 103).

In these passages the moral disposition is associated so closely with the "heart" that they form
one compound noun. The faith that Kant commends is
one that is based on the "pure disposition of the
heart", and it is by virtue of the "pure moral disposition of the heart" that man is pleasing to God.
The heart is by tradition the organ of feeling, of
man's emotional life as distinct from his intellect;
yet the disposition is now actually referred to in
terms of the heart, as when Kant speaks of a complete "change of heart" as necessary if a sinner is
to obtain forgiveness from God.

Hitherto the "heart" has been associated in
Kant's moral philosophy with those feelings and inclinations of the empirical world which he regards
as posing a threat to the pure moral law. In the
"Critique" for instance he takes exception to the
feeling of "pity" and "soft-hearted sympathy", the
"weichherzige Teilnehmung", if it tends to usurp the
function of the sense of duty, and interferes with
the moral law as laid down by reason (V.118,222).

Even in the "Religion", where Kant introduces
his new concept of the "heart" in association with
the moral disposition, it is still possible to find
the earlier pejorative type of reference to the empirical heart, as we see from the following passage.
-"Wenn andre Triebfedern nötig sind, die Willkür zu
gesetzmäßigen Handlungen zu bestimmen, als das Gesetz selbst (z.B.Ehrbegierde, Selbstliebe überhaupt,
ja gar gutherziger Instinkt, dergleichen das Mitleid
ist), so ist es bloß zufällig, daß diese mit dem Gesetz übereinstimmen; denn sie könnten eben sowohl
zur Übertretung antreiben." -"If motives other than
the law itself are necessary to determine the will
to perform actions which conform to the law (e.g. a
desire for honour, self-love in general, even kind-
hearted instinct, such as pity), then it is merely
a matter of chance if these agree with the law; for
they might just as well lead to transgression of the
law" (VI.30f). In this passage the "heart", which is
kind (literally "good"), because it feels pity, is

not considered by Kant to be morally good, since the emotion which it feels is merely "instinctive"; it is not an emotion which is influenced by rational or moral considerations. As we have already suggested, this is a view which could justifiably be challenged on the ground that the person who feels pity does in fact stand back from his emotion and so to speak give it the approval of his moral self before acting on it. As we are reminded by Schiller, nature (in the sense of pure natural feeling), is never merely nature, for it is part of the total life of the soul.

We have seen that the second of the two archetypal principles, the immanent moral principle, so far referred to as the "good" will, or the moral predisposition ("Anlage"), or above all the moral disposition ("Gesinnung"), is now sometimes referred to as the "heart". The first of the two archetypal moral principles, transcendent in relation to the immanent principle, has been exemplified by reason and moral law, or (in the "Dialectic" and the "Religion") by God himself, or (in the "Religion") by the "elective will".

Why does the relation between these two archetypal principles continually recur under different names? Why is the distinction between them so fundamental? Perhaps because they correspond to the two principles involved in the basic division between man's intelligence and his human nature, his conscious existence and his instinctive existence, his reason and his feeling. But that is the one form in which Kant will not express this fundamental relation; for he will not identify the immanent moral principle with man's "feelings", nor with his "sensuous" existence, nor with human nature as such. He will identify the immanent moral principle with the "good" will or with the moral "Gesinnung", but he will not identify it with the empirical aspect of human existence. Despite the dependence of moral law on the empirical world where it is to be put into practice, Kant will not allow the world of pure reason to be corrupted, as he fears, by empiricism. The empirical world and the rational-moral world must remain for ever apart. It is understood that the "good" will in the "Foundations" is on the rational-moral side of the great divide, and so too is the moral "disposition" in the "Critique" and the "Religion".

But now the term chosen by Kant to represent principle (b), the immanent moral disposition, is the "heart", an expression sometimes employed in reference to certain empirical feelings and natural inclinations, which in Kant's view deprive man of his autonomy; for when he is in the grip of such an inclination, or of some desire for an object, it is as though he were acting in accordance, not with his own will, his own law, but with some other law; and therefore such action is described as heteronomous.

It is almost as though a "fault" in the geological sense had occurred in the philosophical structure of Kant's thought, as though the strata of such concepts as "nature", "heart" and "feeling" had suddenly been displaced and were now lying side by side with such strata as reason, transcendence and the unconditional. On the other hand we must not overlook the possibility that the "heart", translated to the rational-moral world, may itself undergo a certain change, so as to adapt it to the values of that world. By elevating the heart above the empirical world to the rational-moral world, Kant draws attention to the fact that even within the rational-moral world he has been operating with an immanent principle, the moral disposition, which is analogous to the pure feeling which, in the opinion of Rousseau and Schiller, is characteristic of human nature.

If the will, instead of being influenced by some inclination alien to its own moral disposition, is on the contrary influenced by its own "Herzensgesinnung", its own "disposition of the heart", this clearly has the most important moral implications. It is the difference between action which is both heteronomous and in conflict with moral law, and action which is both autonomous and moral.

Kant's concept of the "heart" has now shifted away from the empirical world toward the rational-moral or "noumenal" end of his philosophical spectrum. This is demonstrated, for instance, by a passage in which Kant first describes a truly virtuous person as "virtuous according to his intelligible character (virtus Noumenon)"; but then goes on to describe the same person in terms of the "change of heart" ("Änderung des Herzens", VI.47) that he has undergone. There is the same implication in a reference to God as penetrating the "intelligible principle of the heart" ("für denjenigen, der den intelligibelen Grund des Herzens...durchschaut", VI.48). As we have seen in the "Critique", the noumenal world is a world in which man is morally free (where he is "determinable by laws which he gives to himself").

The idea of entrusting moral principles to the "heart", which would have been anathema to Kant when he wrote his previous mature works, is now acceptable. Edification, he says, "gelingt nicht anders, als daß man systematisch zu Werke geht, feste Grundsätze...tief ins Herz legt" (VI.198). Indeed, the suggestion that moral principles need to be implanted deep in the human heart if they are to be effective, is reminiscent of Schiller's statement (in the fourth of the "Letters on the Aesthetic Education of Man", NA.315) that "if we are to rely upon man's moral conduct as we do on natural effects, it must itself be nature".

In view of the obvious difference between the philosophy of Kant and that of Rousseau, the former stressing mainly reason, and the latter stressing the pure feelings of the human heart, it might seem to be an indication of the change that has overtaken Kant's philosophy, that the passages in which he refers both to reason and to the heart should resemble so closely corresponding references in Rousseau. In one such passage the light of reason is associated by Rousseau with the warmth of the heart ("Eclairons sa raison de nouvelles lumières, échauffons son cœur de nouveaux sentiments",CEV.1.454). Natural law,says

Rousseau in another passage (CEV.1.294), is both inscribed in human reason and also engraved indelibly
in the heart of man; and it was perhaps only to be
expected that Rousseau, in this passage, would describe the impression made by natural law on the
heart as the more lasting of the two. -"Si la loi
naturelle n'était écrite que dans la raison humaine,
elle serait peu capable de diriger la plupart de nos
actions. Mais elle est encore gravée dans le cœur de
l'homme en caractères ineffacables" (CEV.1.294).Kant
might not have altogether agreed with Rousseau on
that point, but at least his adoption of the concept
of the heart shows that he wishes to make it clear
that reason as an instrument of the divine will is
incomplete without the moral disposition, i.e. without a principle that is analogous to the "heart".

But as we have already seen, the "heart" to which
Kant is now willing to entrust moral principles is
the heart which is referred to as the "intelligible"
principle of the heart. It is the heart in which the
will of God himself is inscribed, through his pure
moral laws ("die reine moralische Gesetzgebung, dadurch der Wille Gottes ursprünglich in unser Herz
geschrieben ist", VI.104). It is the heart in which
the precepts of duty have been inscribed by reason
("die Vorschriften der Pflicht, wie sie ursprünglich
ins Herz des Menschen durch die Vernunft geschrieben
sind", V.84).

It is the concept of the heart which underlies
Kant's account of a truly ethical community, which
as he points out is not based on any hierarchical
structure, ruled over by a Pope or by patriarchs,
bishops or prelates (VI.102). Kant goes on to describe his concept of an ethical community in the
following terms. -"It would be best to compare an
ethical community with a domestic fellowship (a family), under a common, although invisible, moral
father, in so far as his holy son, who knows his
will, and who at the same time is related by blood
with all the other members, is his representative,
making known his will to the others, who therefore

honour the Father in him, and so together form a voluntary, universal and enduring union of hearts" (VI.102). -"Ein ethisches, gemeines Wesen...würde noch am besten mit der einer Hausgenossenschaft (Familie) unter einem gemeinschaftlichen, obzwar unsichtbaren, moralischen Vater verglichen werden können, sofern sein heiliger Sohn, der seinen Willen weiß und zugleich mit allen ihren Gliedern in Blutsverwandtschaft steht, die Stelle desselben darin vertritt, daß er seinen Willen diesen näher bekannt macht, welche daher in ihm den Vater ehren und so untereinander in eine freiwillige, allgemeine und fortdauernde Herzensvereinigung treten."

The description of the ethical community in terms of a family, contrasted as it is with a church ruled over by powerful dignitaries, calls to mind the passage in the first version of the "Social Contract", in which Rousseau compares the head of a family with a head of State (CEV.463). It is a comparison which is all in favour of the head of a family, just as Kant's comparison is all in favour of the ethical community, ruled over by God the Father. In Rousseau the immediacy or intimacy of the relationship between the members of the family is based on their blood-relationship and their mutual affection. In Kant's description of the ethical community God is honoured by his family in his son Jesus. Rousseau describes the head of State as remote from his subjects and as seeing them only through the eyes of his officials, while the father of a family "sees everything himself". God, described by Kant as "invisible", might appear to be too remote to have such an intimate relation with his human family; but in the "union of hearts" ("Herzensvereinigung") which Kant refers to, God as one who knows the heart of man (he is the "Herzenskündiger") has a far more intimate knowledge of his family than any earthly father.

As Kant says in another passage, the lawgiver of the ethical community can be none other than God himself; for the duties of the community are framed in his commandments; and he, who (as we are again reminded) knows the human heart, can alone search the inmost disposition of each individual. "Also kann nur ein solcher als oberster Gesetzgeber eines ethischen gemeinen Wesens gedacht werden, in Ansehung dessen alle wahren Pflichten, mithin auch die ethischen, zugleich als seine Gebote vorgestellt werden müssen; welcher daher auch ein Herzenskündiger sein muß, um auch das Innerste der Gesinnungen eines jeden zu durchschauen..." (VI.99).

Despite the "universal" character of the ethical community, it is also "freiwillig", that is, voluntary or spontaneous. So the ethical community is contrasted with the "repressed" condition of a church subject to an "authoritarian" form of government. Thus Kant in the "Religion" emphasises the immanent presence of God, just as in the "Foundations" he demonstrated the presence in man of an immanent moral principle.

We have not yet exhausted the significance of Kant's concept of the "heart". He speaks of a bad heart, as well as of a good heart, and this does not simply imply the distinction between a good and a bad propensity. Kant speaks of a bad heart as deceiving itself, as throwing dust in its own eyes, as pretending to act from a morally good motive, when in fact its motive is a selfish one. If this happens, we are unable to establish within ourselves a "sincere moral disposition". ("Diese Unredlichkeit, welche die Gründung echter moralischer Gesinnung in uns abhält...", VI.38.) A good disposition is always in danger of falling into bad ways, unless it has the ability to examine its own motives, and to choose to act only from a motive which it sincerely believes to be morally good. A corrupt or perverse heart will prefer a motive which is not morally good, or sometimes the fragility of the heart is such that, even when it has adopted the moral law as its motive, it yields to some other motive (VI.29f). Again, the "impurity" of the human heart sometimes causes it to be influenced by some other motive, as

well as by that of the moral law, with the result
that actions which conform to the law are not carried out purely from respect for, or in the spirit
of the law (VI.30). A good heart must have the consciousness to choose the good motive as opposed to
the bad one - a choice which it must exercise with
the utmost truthfulness and sincerity. That is why,
in the first reference to the "heart" in the "Religion", the ability or inability of the elective will
to adopt the moral law as its maxim, is described in
terms of "the good or the bad heart".

"Man kann noch hinzusetzen, daß die aus dem
natürlichen Hange entspringende Fähigkeit oder Un-
fähigkeit der Willkür,das moralische Gesetz in seine
Maxime aufzunehmen oder nicht, das gute oder das
böse Herz genannt werde" (VI.29).

The heart as described by Kant in the section
entitled "Man is by nature bad" (VI.32) is not simply a disposition which automatically obeys the moral law. It is in the depth of the heart that a moral
battle is fought between a tendency to decide in
favour of "self-love" and a tendency to conquer the
perversity of the heart, and to choose morality. The
"good" heart, if it prevails, may outwardly appear
to be simply a good disposition which naturally
obeys moral law. But Kant seems to imply that the
heart is "elective", just as the "Willkür" is. If
the "goodness" of the heart prevails, it does so,
not simply as principle (b), the moral disposition,
but also as principle (a), a rational-moral principle like the elective will, a principle which in the
depths of the conscience has elected to renounce its
perverse predilection for self-love, and has consciously chosen to act on moral law. It is precisely
because the heart also has a propensity to evil,
that it cannot simply be a disposition. It seems to
be implied that it must rise above the level of a
disposition, become a will, and declare in favour of
the good disposition as against the bad one.

Kant's description of God as one who knows the
human heart itself implies that God judges the heart

according to the way in which it discharges its responsibility for choosing the right motive. There
would be no point in speaking of a God who knows and
judges the human heart, if the heart were capable of
adopting the moral law by its very nature, and without having to make a conscious decision to do so.
There would be no merit in its adopting the moral
law as its maxim, and no demerit in its adopting another maxim, if it had no freedom of choice and did
not need to exercise its sense of responsibility in
coming to a decision. Merit or demerit arises, in
the eyes of God, only when the heart is free either
to accept or to reject the moral law, and when the
acceptance or rejection of the moral law is the work
of the heart itself. Furthermore, if the heart is
now to be regarded as not merely a disposition, but
also as an "elective" principle, this serves to dif-
ferentiate it even more from the "empirical" heart,
as viewed by Kant.

Paradoxically enough Kant, having introduced
the concept of the heart in order to take account of
the affective aspect of the subjective moral disposition, then proceeds to intellectualise it, lest he
should forfeit the rational basis of his moral philosophy. In this we have yet another example of the
tension in his philosophy between his aim of bridg-
ing the gulf between the rational-moral world and
the empirical world, and on the other hand the need
to keep the two worlds apart. Yet at the same time
he strives for a synthesis of principle (a) and
principle (b), by demonstrating logically and convincingly that the moral "disposition" as such (an
immanent principle) is not self-sufficient unless it
is also an "elective" principle, consciously and
rationally choosing moral motives, and rejecting
immoral motives, as a basis for action.

The use of the concept of the "heart" in con-
junction with that of the moral disposition, tends
to suggest a certain analogy between the "Herzensgesinnung" and Schiller's principle of "pure nature".
Normally, however, Kant is disinclined to draw the
reader's attention to this analogy, for obvious

reasons, such as his doubts about the moral status of Schiller's principle and his own desire to safeguard the rational-moral principle from empiricism.

However, there is one occasion when Kant is unable to avoid discussing the analogy between the moral disposition and Schiller's principle of pure nature. This occasion is his reply to Schiller's criticism of the rigorism that is conspicuous in his moral philosophy. Indeed, Kant can scarcely avoid the subject when, accused by Schiller of moral rigorism, he needs to refute the charge by appealing to the spontaneity of just such a principle as the moral disposition.

We have already referred to the passage (V.118, 222,supra 80) in which Kant first concedes that "an inclination to duty" may facilitate the effectiveness of moral maxims, but then adds that such an inclination cannot by itself produce moral action. Schiller appears to quote from this passage in his treatise "On Grace and Dignity" (NA.283), where he uses the reference to an "inclination to duty" to underline his own belief that "it is only by the participation of his inclination in his moral action that the moral perfection of man can be made apparent" ("daß die sittliche Vollkommenheit des Menschen gerade nur aus dem Anteil seiner Neigung an seinem moralischen Handeln erhellen kann"). "Not virtues, but virtue is his principle", Schiller continues, "and virtue is nothing but an 'inclination to duty'" ("Nicht Tugenden, sondern die Tugend ist seine Vorschrift, und Tugend ist nichts anders 'als eine Neigung zu der Pflicht'",ibid). Schiller's point is that the essence of virtue is to be found, not simply in the performance of outward acts of morality, but rather in the presence within man of an inner virtuous inclination. Whereas in Schiller's opinion man's whole being, his pure natural inclinations as well as his reason, should be involved in his moral conduct, in Kant's view (as interpreted by Schiller) it is from reason alone that moral conduct can arise; and even if natural inclination may sometimes

appear to play a part in assisting reason, such inclination is really only the subjective aspect of
the determination of the will by reason and moral
law. In view of Kant's negative attitude to "inclinations", whether this expression refers to the selfish or the pure natural inclinations, and in view
also of the fact that Schiller's philosophy is based
precisely on the part played by the pure natural inclinations in cooperating with the moral principles
formulated by reason, it is not surprising that in
his treatise "On Grace and Dignity" Schiller should
have criticised Kant for his critical attitude to
the concept of pure nature. Schiller condemns the
austerity that Kant displays in representing natural
inclinations as a threat to the moral law based on
reason (NA.284); he refers to Kant's "Draconian"
moral philosophy ("Er war der Drako seiner Zeit",
NA.285); and he complains that through the imperative form of the moral law mankind is "arraigned and
humiliated" in Kant's philosophy (NA.289). When
Schiller, in his treatise, declares that "man must
obey his reason with joy" (NA.283), he is referring
to his belief that man, endowed as he is with a pure
natural inclination, cannot but joyfully acclaim the
morality which arises from his pure reason. "Only
when it issues from his total humanity as the combined effect of both principles, only when it has
become second nature to him, is his morality secure"
(ibid). But as we have seen, this belief of Schiller in "pure nature" as a principle which reinforces
the morality of pure reason, is rejected by Kant as
empirical in origin.

Schiller justifiably criticises Kant's tendency
to discredit man's pure natural inclinations simply
by lumping them together with his cruder or more
selfish kind of inclination. "Because impure inclinations often usurp the name of virtue, did that justify bringing suspicion upon the unselfish emotion
in the noblest breast?" (NA.285). -"Weil oft sehr
unreine Neigungen den Namen der Tugend usurpieren,
mußte darum auch der uneigennützige Affekt in der
edelsten Brust verdächtig gemacht werden?" With the

purest, the noblest emotion Kant also tends to reject the artistic inclination, so closely related to
the pure inclination. As Schiller complains: "In the
Kantian moral philosophy the idea of duty is expounded with a severity that frightens away the Graces".
-"In der Kantischen Moralphilosophie ist die Idee
der Pflicht mit einer Härte vorgetragen, die alle
Grazien davon zurückschreckt" (NA.284).

In the footnote to VI.23 Kant gives the following reply to Schiller's criticism.

"Professor Schiller in his masterly treatise...
on "Grace and Dignity" in morality, disapproves of
this way of representing obligation, as though it
implied a Carthusian (ascetic) disposition of the
soul; but since we are in agreement in the most important principles, I cannot concede that we are in
disagreement on this point, if only we can make our
meaning clear to each other. I readily admit that
the concept of duty, precisely on account of its
Dignity, is not to be associated with Grace. For
Duty implies unconditional constraint, a concept to
which Grace is directly opposed. The majesty of the
Law (like that on Sinai) inspires reverence (not
fear which repels, nor charm which invites famili-
arity), but Respect felt by him who receives the law
for him who gives it; though in this case, since the
latter is to be found in ourselves, the law arouses
a sense of the sublimity of our destiny, which up-
lifts us more than any beauty. But Virtue, that is
to say, the firmly established disposition to fulfil
one's Duty punctiliously, is in its consequences not
less beneficent, indeed more so than anything which
Nature or Art can accomplish; and the glorious image
of humanity exhibited in this form consorts well
with the companionship of the Graces, who nevertheless, when it is simply a question of Duty, keep
themselves at a respectful distance. Only when we
consider the graceful effect which Virtue,if it were
everywhere accepted, would diffuse throughout the
world, would morally inspired Reason, by its power
of imagination, admit the claims of sensibility.

Only after his conquest of the monsters does Hercules become the leader of the Muses; before that labour the good sisters shrink back. These attendants of Venus Urania are but courtesans in the train of Venus Dione, as soon as they meddle in the business of Duty, and presume to provide the motives thereto. Now if one asks what is the aesthetic quality, so to speak the temperament of Virtue, spirited and therefore joyous, or bowed down by anxiety and dejected, it is scarcely necessary to answer. The latter slavish condition of the soul can never be present without a secret hatred of the law; and cheerfulness of heart in discharging one's duty (not complacency in recognising it) proclaims the sincerity of one's virtuous disposition, even in the case of piety, which consists, not in the repentant sinner's self-torment (which is most ambiguous, and is commonly only an inner reproach at having offended against the rules of prudence), but rather in the firm resolution to do better in the future; a resolution which, when encouraged by good progress, must produce a joyful mood of the soul, without which one is never certain that one has learned to love goodness, i.e. has taken it up into one's maxim."

Despite the urbanity and the conciliatory nature of his reply, Kant makes scarcely any concessions. When Schiller criticises him for his negative attitude to natural inclinations, he replies that there must be rigorism in the application of the moral law, implying of course that natural inclinations must not be allowed to come between us and our moral duty. If it is a question of duty, any admixture of the qualities associated with "grace" (natural inclinations, however "pure") is to be deprecated, since duty calls for "unconditional constraint" ("unbedingte Nötigung"), to be imposed on even the purer type of natural inclination. In other words, natural inclinations must not be allowed to trespass within the province of morality. The proper attitude to the majesty of the law, such as that on Mount Sinai, is one of reverence and respect.

If Kant is not disposed to make concessions to Schiller, this is because he has no need to do so. All that he must do is to point to two features of his moral philosophy which Schiller appears to have overlooked, or at least has not mentioned. In the first place, even in the field of reason and moral law, there is one feature of Kant's philosophy to which Schiller's complaint concerning rigorism does not apply. Kant's rigorism is relieved by the principle of autonomy, since it is our own reason which produces the moral law for us; and it is when we are able to associate our self, not with our natural inclinations, but with a moral law produced by our own reason, that we experience a sense of the "sublimity" of our own moral destiny. Kant, by referring to "ein Gefühl des Erhabenen unserer eigenen Bestimmung", reminds Schiller of this feature of his moral philosophy.

Kant might also have referred to the key passage in the "Foundations" (432,90,supra 36f) where he gives the most convincing account of the way in which the moral law, ideally, according to the principle of autonomy, arises spontaneously from man's own will, and is for that very reason "unconditional", because he is himself inwardly committed to it, as he could not be if it were simply imposed on him.

But it is in the second part of his reply that Kant introduces his main argument, based on the moral disposition. Duty may sometimes call for "unconditional constraint", but at other times, Kant suggests, duty is best entrusted to "virtue", which he defines as "the firmly established disposition to fulfil one's duty punctiliously" ("die Tugend, d.i. die fest gegründete Gesinnung seine Pflicht genau zu erfüllen").

There is scope for spontaneity in the second archetypal principle, the moral disposition; for it is important that the impulse to act in accordance with and for the sake of moral law should spring spontaneously from one's own subjective moral disposition. It is mainly to the immanent principle of the moral "Gesinnung" that Kant appeals in seeking

to exonerate himself from the charge of rigorism, a
charge brought against him on the ground that he repudiates the pure emotions of the human heart, that
is, pure nature. The passage affords us a unique in-
sight into Kant's view of the part played by the
"Herzensgesinnung" as compared with that which is
assigned to the principle of pure nature in Schiller's philosophy. Both are subjective moral principles, both operate spontaneously through feeling
(the heart), both serve to inspire action in the
spirit of the moral law; and both can therefore be
regarded as fulfilling the same function. In speaking of "Nature or Art", Kant makes a fairly explicit
reference to Schiller's principle of pure nature,
which he represents in his treatise as capable of
being cultivated by means of art. The voluntarism
which Kant associates with the moral disposition is
further emphasised by the reference to the "joyful
heart" which in fulfilling its duty vindicates the
"sincerity of the virtuous disposition" ("das fröhliche Herz in Befolgung seiner Pflicht...ist ein
Zeichen der Echtheit tugendhafter Gesinnung"); and
by the reference to the "joyful mood of the soul
without which one is never certain that one has
learned to love goodness" ("eine fröhliche Gemüts-
stimmung...ohne welche man nie gewiß ist, das Gute
auch lieb gewonnen...zu haben").

So we see that when Schiller reproaches Kant
with neglecting or repudiating the pure natural inclinations, Kant replies by appealing to his own
principle of the moral disposition,a principle which
he is now referring to as the "Herzensgesinnung",
the "disposition of the heart", and which he claims
is just as spontaneous and unconstrained as Schiller's principle of pure nature. By invoking his own
principle of the "Gesinnung" in defending himself
against Schiller's criticism, Kant produces a sound
and convincing argument based on the moral disposition. He blunts the thrust of Schiller's criticism,
not by unjustifiably denying the charge of rigorism
in rejecting natural inclinations (which would have

played into the hands of the revisionists), but by producing the moral disposition as a counterweight to Schiller's principle of pure nature.

However, although Kant is prepared to compare the moral disposition with pure nature, he does so without prejudice to his main position, based as it is on the belief that the former principle, belonging to the rational-moral order, is superior to a principle belonging to the empirical world. After asserting that the "Gesinnung" is "in its effect also beneficent" ("Aber die Tugend, die fest gegründete Gesinnung seine Pflicht genau zu erfüllen, ist in ihren Folgen auch wohltätig"), he then claims that the moral disposition is in fact more beneficent than "nature or art" ("mehr wie Alles,was Natur oder Kunst in der Welt leisten mag"), which as we have seen is a reference to pure nature. So Kant, even while comparing the moral disposition with pure nature, at the same time asserts its superiority to that empirical principle.

The same thing applies to the idea of an "inclination to duty", to which each of the two philosophers adopts his own characteristic attitude. We have noted the passage in which Kant concedes that an "inclination to duty" may facilitate the effectiveness of moral maxims without actually producing any (supra p.80). We have also noted that Schiller in his treatise seizes upon Kant's reference to an "inclination to duty" in order to develop his own more positive attitude to what is obviously a moral inclination. "Virtue", says Schiller,"is nothing but an 'inclination to duty'" (supra p.123). As we have seen, Kant in his reply to Schiller refers to Virtue as "the disposition to fulfil one's duty punctiliously" ("die fest gegründete Gesinnung seine Pflicht genau zu erfüllen"). So Kant converts Schiller's "natural inclination" to duty, to his own rational-moral "disposition" to fulfil one's duty.

In his reply to Schiller's criticism Kant employs two distinct concepts of "duty". In the first place he associates this concept with "Dignity" or reason.

He therefore has to dissociate it from "Grace", or by implication from pure natural inclination. "Ich gestehe gern: daß ich dem Pflichtbegriffe gerade um seiner Würde willen keine Anmut beigesellen kann. Denn er enthält unbedingte Nötigung" (VI.23fn). According to this first concept of Duty it implies "unconditional constraint" applied by reason and moral law to a will which is subject to crude or selfish inclinations. In the second place when Kant speaks of virtue in terms of a "firmly established disposition to fulfil one's duty punctiliously" (ibid), he implies that duty depends, not on the "constraint" applied by reason, but rather on the impulse arising from the subjective disposition.

Perhaps it would be true to say that the character or quality of duty depends upon whether we can identify our self with it. In his apostrophe to Duty ("Pflicht! du erhabener, großer Name!",V.86,193) Kant makes what we might call the authoritarian concept of duty almost attractive, because we associate ourselves with its sublimity in raising man (as belonging to the sensible world) above himself. -"Es kann nichts Anderes sein, als was den Menschen über sich selbst (als einen Teil der Sinnenwelt) erhebt."

If on the other hand we feel that duty exerts a certain "constraint" on us, then we react to it negatively; and since it is easier for us to identify ourselves with our "own" inner moral disposition, the concept of duty based on the latter principle is usually the more attractive of the two; which is the reason why Kant, in his reply to Schiller, speaks of "the joyful heart in pursuance of its duty" (VI.24fn). Indeed in some passages the second concept of duty, based on the immanent moral principle as distinct from transcendent reason, is shown to be not only more "joyful", but also ethically more sincere. An outstanding example of this concept of duty is to be found in the passage in the "Dialectic" (V.147,248), where it is illustrated negatively in the case in which we are granted direct knowledge of God. Confronted as we would be with the

awe-inspiring presence of God, we would in Kant's
view obey the law in most cases from a sense of fear
rather than a sense of duty, and therefore our actions would be morally worthless, because in the giv-
en circumstances the spur of action would be external, which would rule out any action from a sense of
duty rooted in our moral disposition. The reader
will recall the more positive account of this type
of duty in the key passage in IV.432,90, which makes
it clear that the only duty that a man can fulfil
unconditionally is the duty that he himself resolves
to fulfil, because it springs from his own indwelling will (supra p.36).

We have seen, particularly in the "Religion",
that Kant seeks to bring his two archetypal principles (principle (a), reason and objective moral law,
and principle (b), the subjective moral disposition)
into closer relationship with each other. It seems
that it is not enough for the "Gesinnung", principle (b), to operate as a "disposition": it must also
operate as an "elective" principle, like the "Willkür" itself, principle (a). Conversely reason and
moral law are incomplete without the support of a
moral principle immanent in the will, a subjective
disposition. There is a complementarity here, a kind
of synthesis, which has a certain analogy with the
synthesis between reason and pure or noble nature
which is accomplished by Schiller in his "Aesthetic
Education of Man".

But Kant rejects the principle of pure nature
as empirical, preferring to operate with the subjective moral disposition immanent in the will; and the
analogy between the syntheses effected by the two
philosophers has to be qualified accordingly. Of the
two principles which are united by Schiller, one is
the rational-moral principle itself, but the other,
pure nature, lies outside the rational-moral system;
and the significance of the synthesis resides precisely in this fact, that it is a genuine union of
opposites, a synthesis of reason and nature.

It is true that Kant operates with a principle,

the moral disposition, which is analogous to pure nature, and that the "heart" in the "Religion" contributes an element of feeling or emotion to the synthesis brought about with reason. But on the other hand the moral disposition, in spite of the analogy with pure nature, belongs in fact to the rational-moral world, and so does the "heart" referred to in the "Religion". The union which Kant seeks to effect between reason and the indwelling moral disposition is a union of two principles which are already, so to speak, on the same side, that is, the rational-moral side.

Nevertheless, even within the rational-moral world, Kant skilfully contrives to bring about a synthesis between principles (a) and (b). These two principles may serve the same end, which is to produce action in the spirit of objective moral law, but they serve it in different ways, the one being transcendent, the other immanent; and the relation between them has a close analogy with that between the two distinct principles of reason and nature. By means of the synthesis of reason with the immanent moral disposition Kant succeeds in giving his moral philosophy a cohesion and a strength which it would otherwise lack. So, with consummate skill, Kant contrives to reconcile two seemingly irreconcilable ends; for he not only preserves the purity of reason from any admixture of empiricism, but he also constructs a bridge, if not between reason and nature, then at least between reason and a principle having a pronounced analogy with pure nature, the immanent principle of the moral disposition.

# BIBLIOGRAPHY

The passages from Kant's works are referred to by the appropriate volume and page in "Kants Gesammelte Schriften", published in Berlin for the Royal Prussian Academy of Sciences by Georg Reimer, 1908.
III. The Critique of Pure Reason.
IV. The Foundations of the Metaphysics of Morals.
V. The Critique of Practical Reason.
VI. Religion within the Limits of Reason.
The translations of passages into English are by the author himself, but the second reference is to the following English version.

Lewis White Beck, the Critique of Practical Reason, and other Writings in Moral Philosophy, translated and edited. University of Chicago Press, Illinois, 1949.

Thus the first reference, IV.393,LWB.55, is to page 393 of "The Foundations" (the German text), followed by the reference to page 55 in the English version. Later in the chapter this might be abbreviated to "393,55".

Other texts. NA: Schillers Werke, Nationalausgabe, Vol.20, Part I, Weimar, 1962.

CEV. - C.E.Vaughan, The Political Writings of Rousseau, Cambridge, 1915.

Commentaries

Richard G.Henson. "What Kant Might Have Said: Moral Worth and the Overdetermination of Dutiful Action". The Philosophical Review, 88 (1979).
Barbara Herman. "On the Value of Acting from the Motive of Duty". The Philosophical Review,90 (1981).
R.B.Louden. "Kant's Virtue Ethics". "Philosophy", 61 (1986).
R.P.Wolff. "The Anatomy of Reason". New York, 1973.

# INDEX